Mark di Suvero

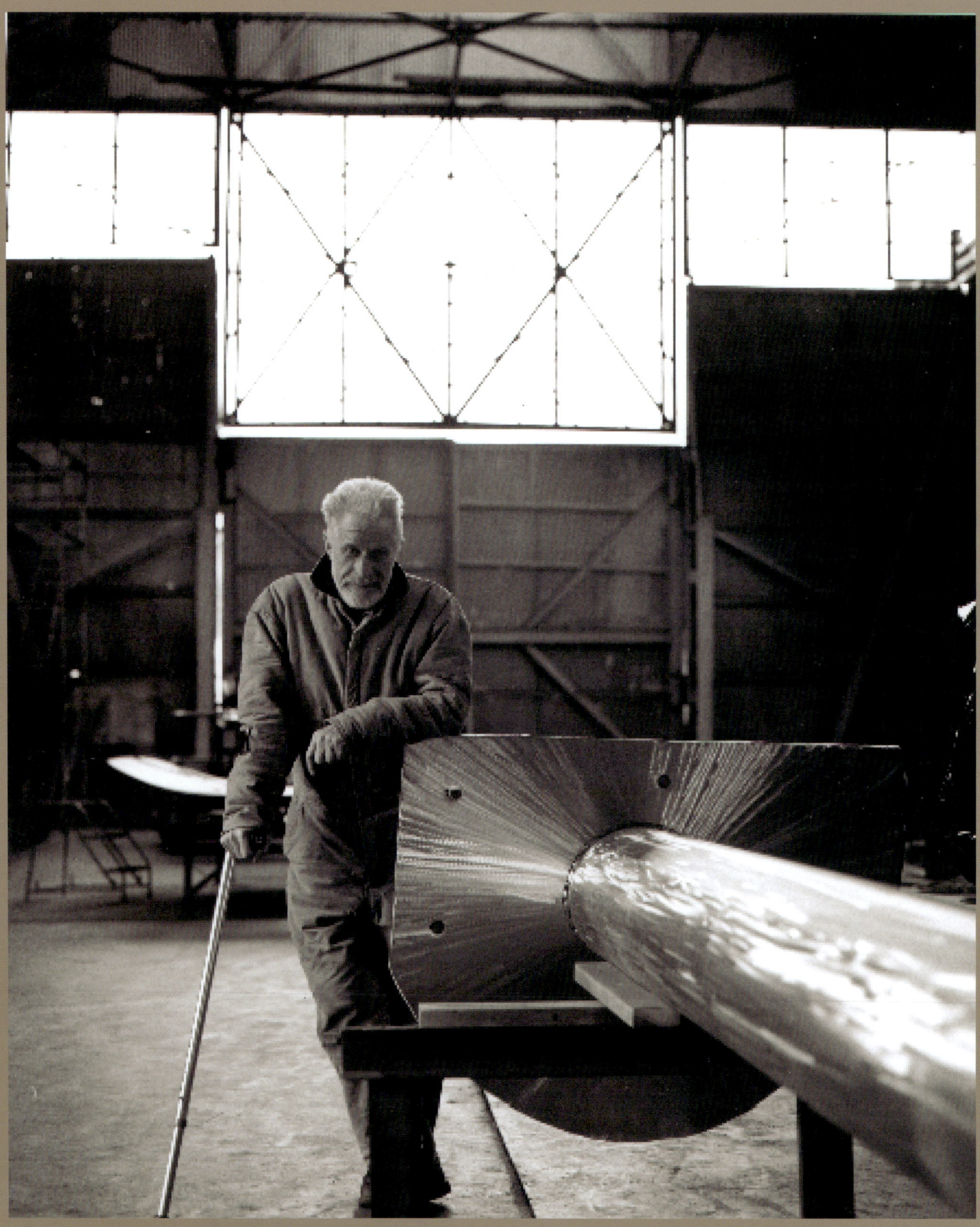

Mark di Suvero in studio

sculpture and drawings

January 28 - March 12, 2011

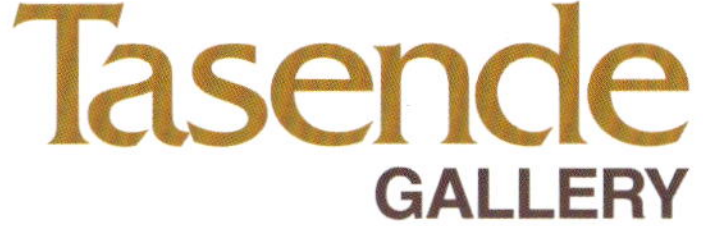

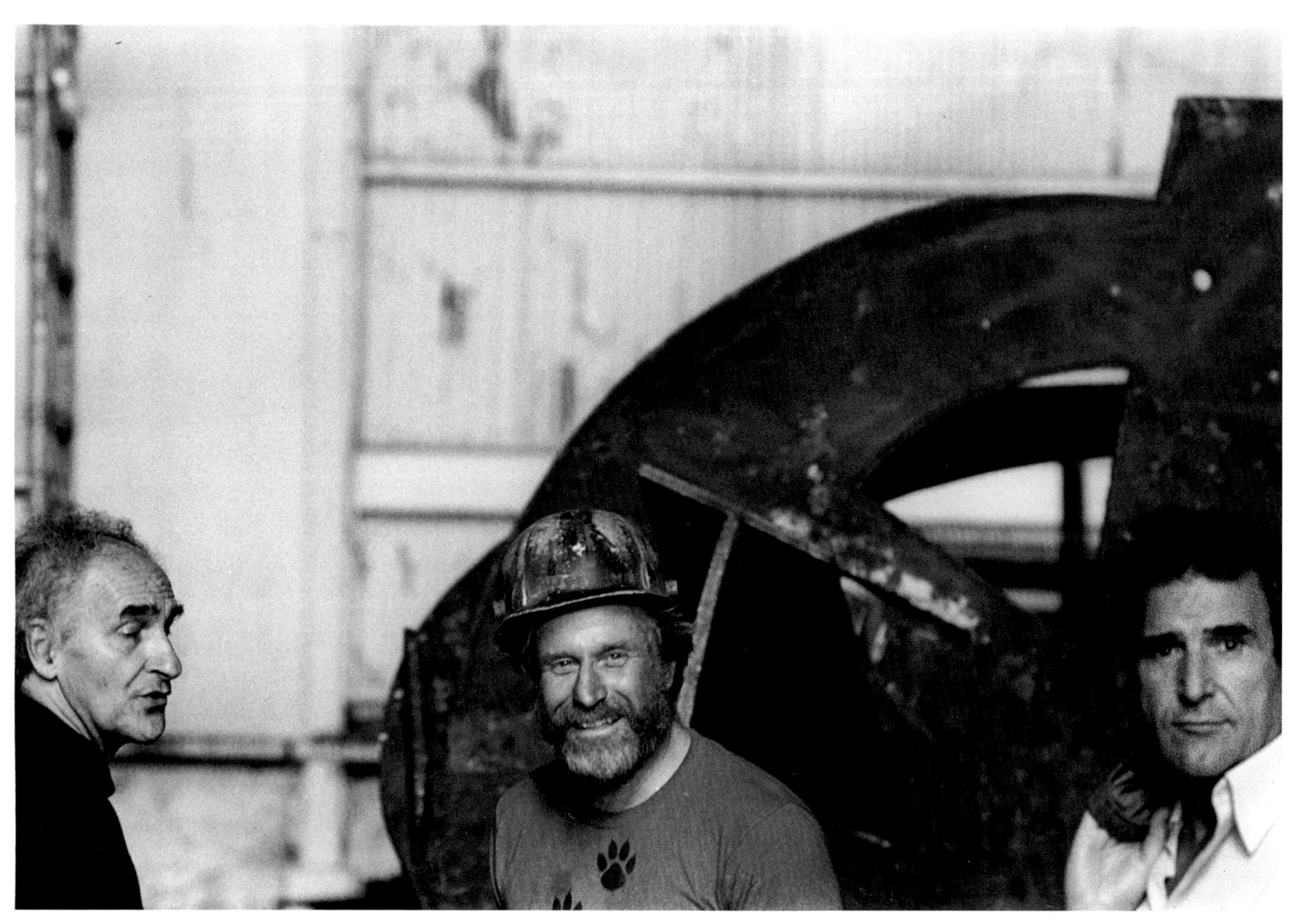

Eduardo Chillida, Mark di Suvero, Jose Tasende, Long Island City, circa 1987

The spacing (e.g., inorganic chemistry) and time (as in the evolution of flight in birds) are dimensions of structure that, like color in flowers, cannot be sub-tracted, seen without. This space-time dimension of structure allows us to see the dynamic continuity between nonlife (the astrophysicist's evolution of stars) and life (the skeletal growth from child to adult in humans).

di Suvero, Mark, and François Barré. *Mark di Suvero Dreambook.* Berkeley: University of California Press. California, 2008, 105. Print.

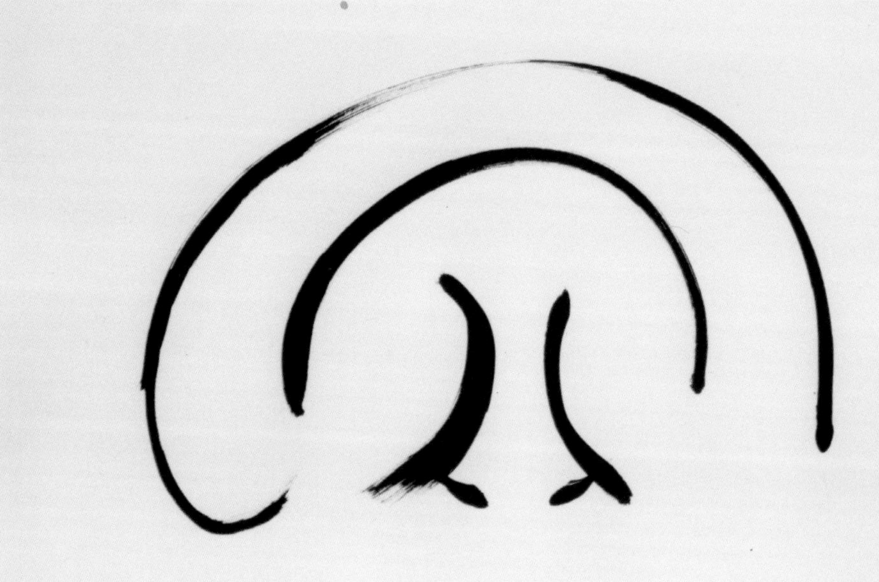

Robert Pincus

State of Being:

THE SINGULAR SCULPTURES OF MARK DI SUVERO

It comes to this: of whatever sort it is

It must be "lit with piercing glances into the life of things":

It must acknowledge the spiritual forces which have made it.

Marianne Moore, the last lines of "When I Buy Pictures"

Mark di Suvero honors many poets in both the titles and spirit of his work. In an elegant catalogue for the 1993 exhibition, *Open Secret: Sculpture, 1990-92*, the text consists of poems that di Suvero had selected to compensate for the inadequacy of photographs to convey how we experience sculpture. "I have thought to add poems I love and that have changed my life," he writes, "so that the bridge between the poem and the photo-image becomes the true reality, a voyage of imagination in your mind's eye."[1] One of those writers is arguably the greatest of American poets, Walt Whitman, who is represented by his beautiful short poem, "A Noiseless Patient Spider," which, in its evocation of "measureless oceans of space" also evokes the soaring nature of the sculpture, *Extase* (1991), on the facing page.

Di Suvero's breakthrough sculpture of 1967 – in his words, "the first truck-crane artist-built sculpture in the United States" – pays homage to one of the great American poets of the 20th century, *Are Years What? (For Marianne Moore).*[2] And in considering di Suvero's large place in the history of American sculpture, we might turn to the words of Moore's great friend and champion, the poet William Carlos Williams. Thinking about how anyone finds a place, or a voice, as a poet, he wrote, "The only way to be like Whitman is to write unlike Whitman."[3] And though Williams' is concerned with poets and poetry, his larger point is about originality, how any artist who wants to create something equal to the artists that inspired him or her, must depart dramatically from them. In part, Williams is surely expressing an anxiety about influence, to paraphrase Harold Bloom; but he is also pointing to the mystery of what makes an artist original and enduring. And there is no doubt that di Suvero, over the course of the last five decades, has demonstrated his ability to resolve this conun-

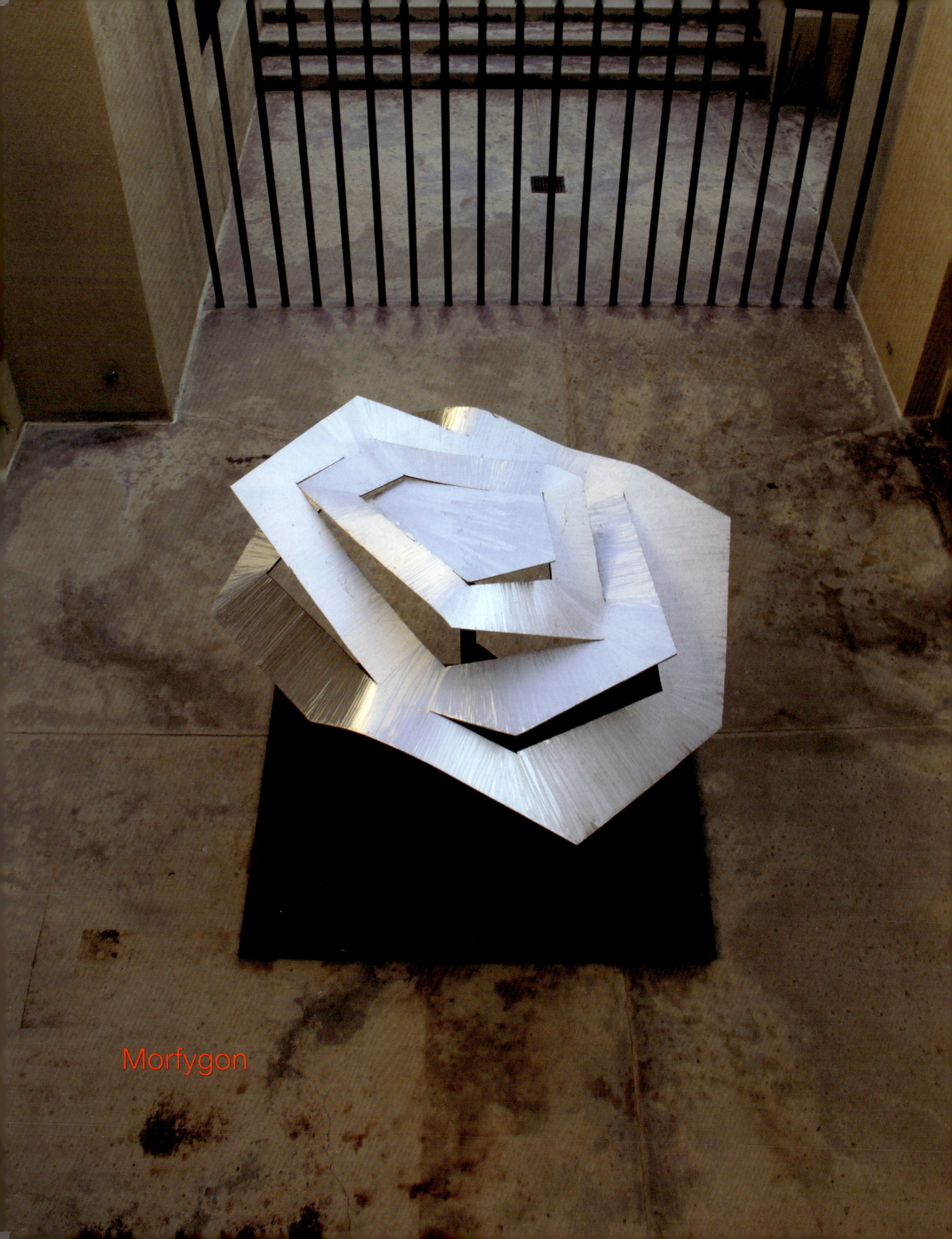

Morfygon

drum concerning the creation of a distinct vision. Looking to a spectrum of sculptors, learning from them, he has also learned how to look beyond them, to forge his own vision of how to work in three dimensions. Turning to another iconic American writer, di Suvero tells as much in his *Dreambook*, writing, "Thoreau taught me: to be original is to see the thing as it is, not as others have told you it is."[4]

Di Suvero's sources are many, as with any true original in any art form. One decisive link is to Abstract Expressionism, David Smith in particular, an influence that di Suvero himself has commented upon. As the late art historian, Irving Sandler, noted, Smith shifted Abstract Expressionist sculpture away from the moribund biomorphic forms of the likes of Herbert Ferber, David Hare, Ibram Lassow, Seymour Lipton and Theodore Roszak and toward a more rigorous use of technology in technique and materials as well as a more taut, vigorous vocabulary of forms. Smith moved sculpture, in di Suvero's words, toward "a really strong, American industrial art."[5] But there was also the example of Smith's New York contemporaries, the Action Painters – Jackson Pollock and Willem de Kooning prime among them – with their freshly dynamic sense of both line and space. The assertive use of black lines to define pictorial place, Franz Kline's specialty, hints at what di Suvero was to accomplish on a far grander scale. But of course di Suvero's influences stretch further in time and geography, to Auguste Rodin, the Russian Constructivists, Alberto Giacometti, Alexander Calder and Julio Gonzalez – all in different ways inspired him by their ability to activate space. Though it is the dramatic presence of di Suvero's forms that commands our attention, it is their relationship to the world around them and the viewer that is paramount to di Suvero. "Space has been the most important element in sculpture for me."[6]

Of course we can take him at his word and still assert that he is being modest. It is in the way he has furthered, in fact has expanded the formal dimensions of modernist sculpture into the 21st century that has made him such a compelling figure. The only other sculptor with a close relationship to Abstract Expressionism whose work has fared as well is John Chamberlain; his use of crushed, smashed and painted metal – whose most famous source is castoff automobile fragments – also has roots in the assemblage movement of the late 1950s and 1960s. Furthermore, Chamberlain didn't have the same penchant for monumentality that he has displayed: scale matters in di Suvero's work. Why else would di Suvero mention the introduction of the crane-built work, as he puts it, among the major events in his "Autobiographical Sketch" in *Dreambook*? The pivotal sculpture to which he refers: *Are Years What? (For Marianne Moore)*. And it's worth looking at a few lines of Moore's poem "What Are Years?" to focus on an essential quality of di Suvero's art. Thinking about a bird, she declares: "Though he is captive, / his mighty singing/says, satisfaction is a lowly/thing, how pure a thing is joy. /This is mortality, / this is eternity."[7] The bird is the poet, too, of course, creating a song that isn't content with mere satisfaction, but is celebrating joy, mortality and eternity. And the sculptor identifies with the bird and his song as well. The bright red, the primary red of the I-beams in di Suvero's homage is a visual analogue to Moore's line "how pure a thing is joy." So, too, is the reach of one long diagonal beam, akin to the neck of a diagrammatic creature. Di Suvero's sculptures often create the impression that they are reaching for the sky, by virtue of their height. (*Are Years What?* stands forty feet tall.) And joy is a recurring term for di Suvero's oeuvre, as the implicitly erotic sculpture, *Joie de Vivre* (1997) affirms.

The joining of mortality and eternity in the poem fits di Suvero's sensibility. His art may be emphatically physical, but there is also a transcendent quality to it. Much as for Thoreau, his touchstone figure for seeing things true, in the everyday world you will find all the signs you need of the spiritual. It's this view that informs another of di Suvero's statements in *Dreambook*, "Something that you, dear reader, should know: that you are God."[8]

It would be misreading this statement to conclude di Suvero is any variety of starry-eyed mystic. As *Dreambook* reveals, he is in equal measure poetic, philosophical, scientific, sociological, political, technological and spiritual in his speculations. And clearly no one who makes monumental sculptures that demonstrates his obvious brilliance in engineering as well as aesthetics is spending all his time dwelling on cosmic matters. Yet it is worth noting that di Suvero's original field of study in college was philosophy, at the University of California, Santa Barbara, and then the University of California in Berkeley, where he completed a B.A. in philosophy in 1956, while also beginning to forge his identity as a sculptor. His writings in *Dreambook* remind us he is still a man of ideas as well as an artist.

His first major forays into sculpture began in the late 1950s, when he moved to New York from Berkeley. His well-known and remarkable works in a Cubist vein made of wood salvaged from destroyed buildings asserted both his ambitions and originality. They also preceded the rise of Minimalism as the dominant movement in sculpture during the 1960s. And while Donald Judd, the major critical voice of Minimalism, would review di Suvero's work favorably, it is worth reminding us that his aesthetic remained distinct from the practices of major Minimalists such as Judd and Carl Andre. The elements in a work by di Suvero are relational, each part relating to the others. The Minimalists' method was modular. As Donald Judd famously described the approach in his essay "Specific Objects," "The order is not rationalistic and underlying but is simply order, like that of continuity, one thing after another."[9]

Order isn't as vital a term in thinking about di Suvero's art. Balance and cogency matter more; so do precision and play. It's not just his mastery of three dimensions that is so difficult to capture in photographs. It's the pleasure of motion that is also missing from images of them. It can be something as simple as a slide, on a massive sculpture named in memory of a beloved dog, *Old Buddy (For Rosko)* (1993-95). Or it can be the sheer beauty of watching a thin, loosely rounded plane of steel shimmer

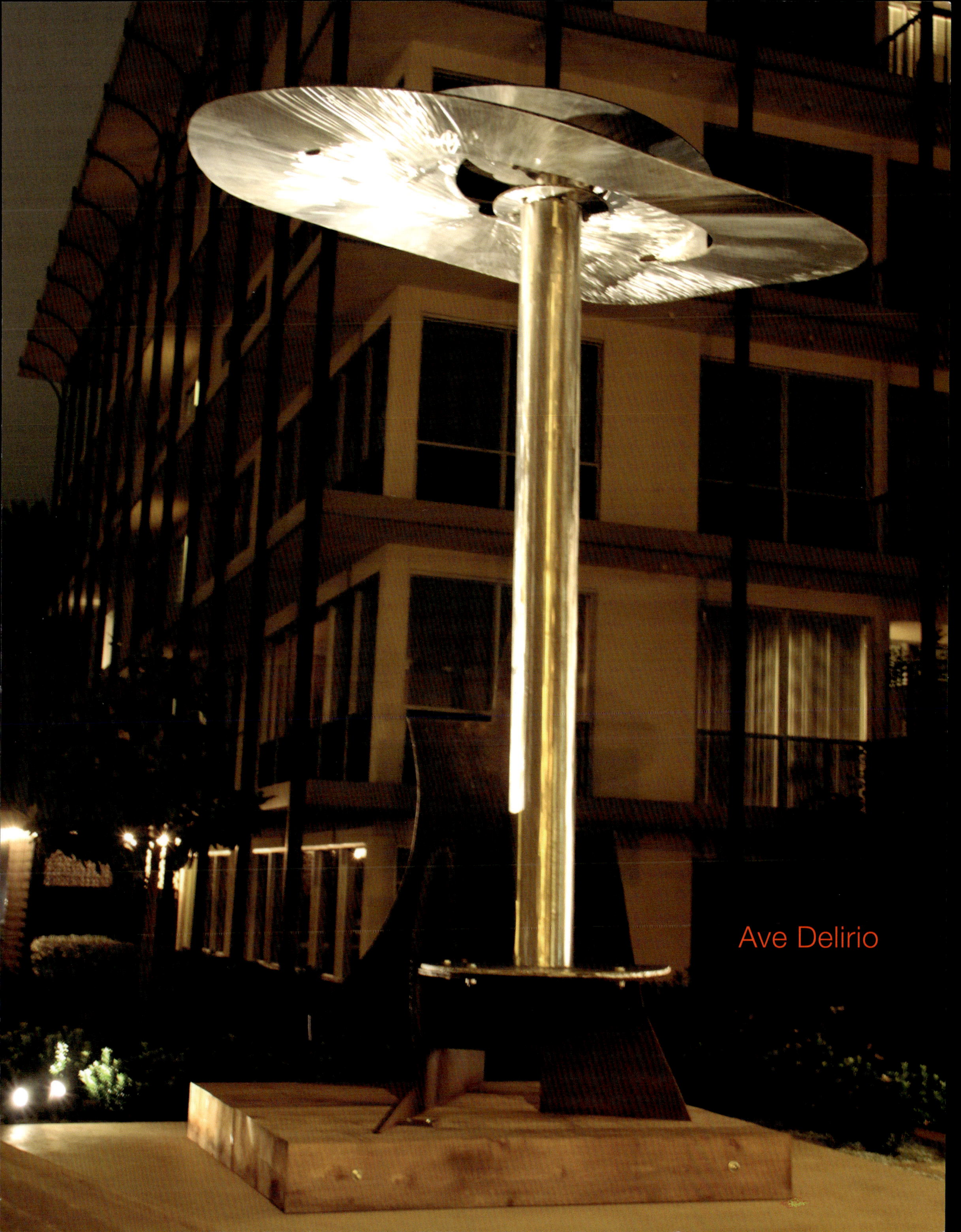
Ave Delirio

as it slowly turns in *Ave Delirio* (2001). Alexander Calder is an inspiration in this respect. "Anybody who does motion in sculpture has to relate to him. Calder's joy is real."[10] But to paraphrase Williams, di Suvero clearly realized that to be like Calder he had to make sculpture unlike Calder.

What he recognized, like Calder before him, is that the pleasure we get from the moving portions of a sculpture is a primal one. It's no coincidence that there was a childlike dimension to Calder's personality and that he was not only the inventor of the mobile but was the creator of the elaborate, miniature *Circus* that holds appeal for children and adults. Di Suvero has been known to invite children into his studio to test some of his work. And he has observed, "Most adults are deficient children; they don't know how to play anymore. The pure response is the child's response."[11] Of course, this comment leaves out the sophisticated understanding of structure in sculpture that makes this possible: to create a place for play requires precision in the work itself. This is evident in all of the large-scale sculptures in this exhibition and some of the small ones.

With a light touch, di Suvero's art heightens our awareness of gravity and balance – preoccupations his work shares with Richard Serra's weighty, ominous Prop sculptures from the 1960s, 1970s and 1980s. Where Serra makes us think about gravity and balance by having steel or lead plates positioned against one another precariously, di Suvero creates forms that seem to float as much as sit at the top of a column. The loftiest work in this respect, of the works on view in the current exhibition, is *Ave Delirio* (2001), nearly 17 and ½ feet tall. Its height seems even greater when the top portion is set in motion, directing our eyes upward. He applies much the same concept in *Morfygon* (2002), but on a human scale; the upper portion, in polished steel, can be set in circular motion. It sits, delicately balanced, on a slender pole. By contrast, *Nextro* (2003) and *Untitled* (2008) each incorporate vertically suspended portions: a curvilinear form within a sphere in the earlier construction; circular bands within circular bands in the later work. In all of these examples, as well as in some of the intimately-sized sculptures on view, such as *Potluck I* (2004), the moving parts are beautifully calibrated. Only an artist who has refined this dimension of his sculptures for decades could make its presence look so inevitable, so intrinsic to the identity of a work. Motion is inseparable from their formal vocabulary, as in Calder's mobiles or the elegant sculptures of George Rickey. The forms themselves are in turn conjoined with the kind of ease that an artist can achieve only after decades of refining his repertoire of forms and materials. His art isn't a case of one thing after another; it's about how one element relates to all those that contribute to the work. And as other works in this exhibition attest, di Suvero is highly comfortable working on a small scale. *Potluck 1* (2004), shaped from small scraps of metal, coheres into an intricate, vertical composition that gently hints at the human figure.

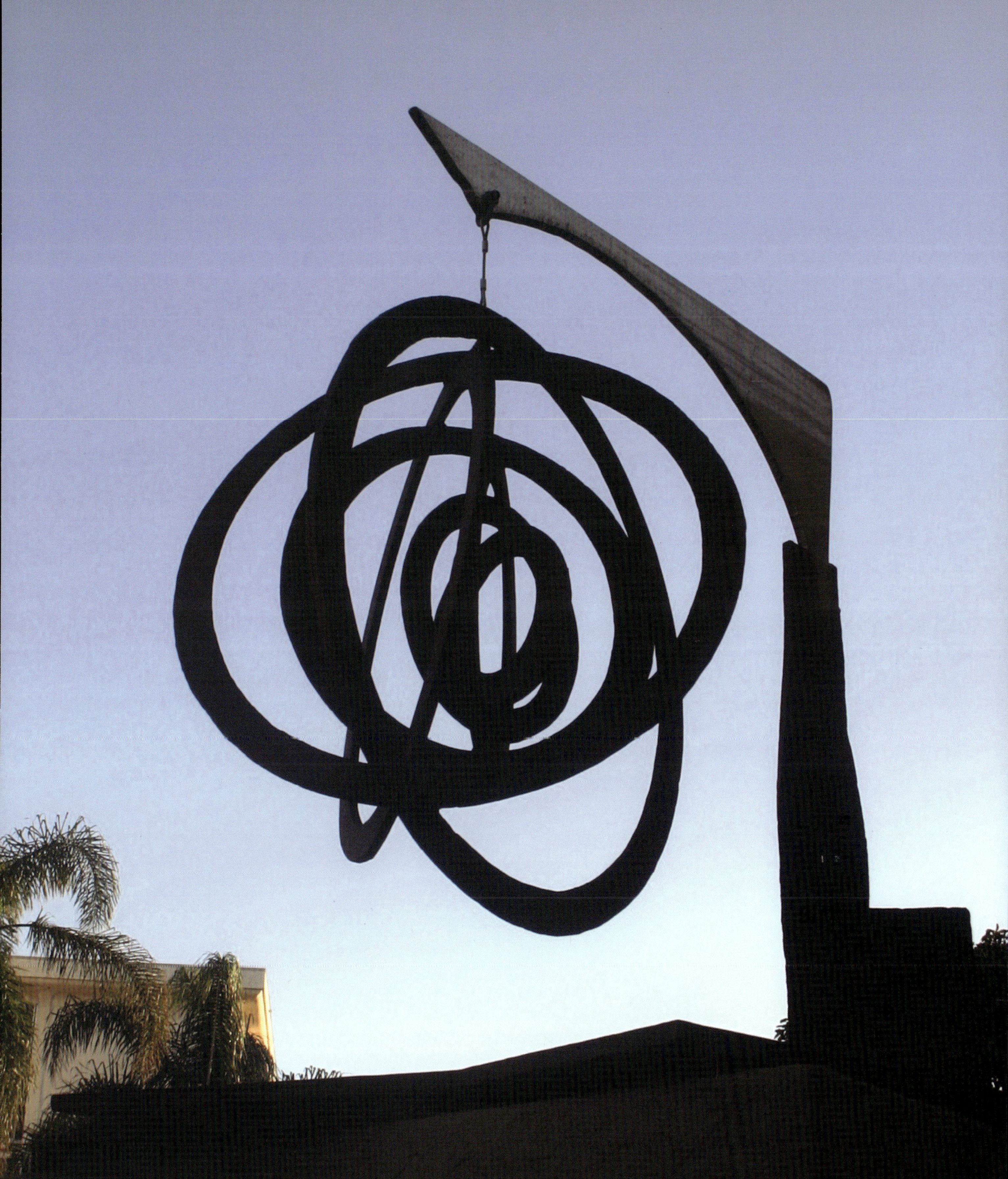

Untitled

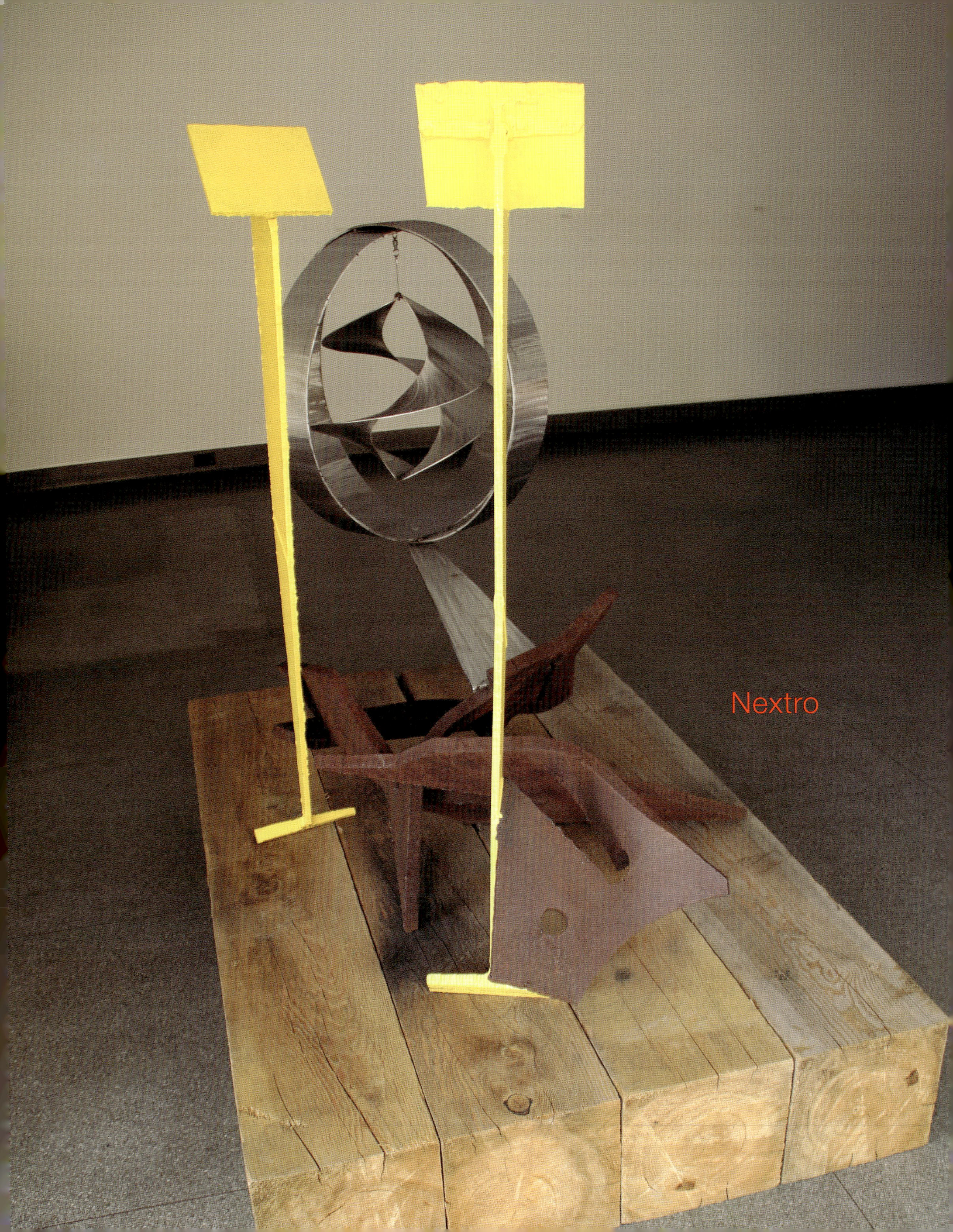

Nextro

Di Suvero has said that the making of sculpture is, for him, akin to "painting in three dimensions."[12] Yet turning that idea on its head, we might see his drawings as two dimensional compositions that imply a third dimension, whether in a spare, calligraphic drawing that reimagines the upper portion of *Ave Delirio* or a densely gathered structure of diagonal bands, organized around a vertical axis, that become a dynamic approximation of a di Suvero sculpture. In either example, it's the grace of the line, the sharp nature of his eye, which is evident.

Using the drawings as a kind of roadmap to the sculptures, it becomes clearer how they mean to occupy physical space with the same imaginative vigor. Installed outside his Long Island City studio, *Ave Delirio* can look striking against the backdrop of the Manhattan skyline. But it looks just as grand in La Jolla, rising above the façade of Tasende Gallery, with the Pacific Ocean stretching out behind it. This sculpture, like innumerable others by him, might be thought of as concretely realized chimeras, abstract visions that occupy real space as surely as we do. In that sense, they are like paintings that have made the passage into our everyday world. But unlike paintings, they persuade us to interact with them – whether simply through viewing them from multiple perspectives, setting in motion their kinetic components, or, in some cases, literally finding places for us on the works themselves. It's as if we were part of the pictures too. Di Suvero's is a generous kind of sculpture, which fulfills his moving notion of art as "a gift we give to others."[13]

Notes

1. Di Suvero, Mark. *Open Secret: Sculpture 1990-92*. New York: Rizzoli International and Gagosian Gallery, 1993. 5. Print.

2. Di Suvero, Mark, and Francois Barré. *Mark Di Suvero: Dreambook*. Berkeley: University of California, 2008. 273. Print.

3. Tashjian, Dickran. *William Carlos Williams and the American Scene, 1920-1940*: Whitney Museum of American Art, December 12, 1978-February 4, 1979: Poems. New York: Whitney Museum of American Art, 1978. 58. Print.

4. Di Suvero, Mark. *Dreambook,* 99. It's worth noting that Thoreau was one of the first and most steadfast admirers of Whitman's *Leaves of Grass*.

5. Di Suvero, Mark, and Irving Sandler. *Mark Di Suvero at Storm King Art Center*. Mountainville, NY.: Storm King Art Center; New York. Harry N. Abrams, 1990. 24-28. Print.

6. Di Suvero, Mark. *Open Secret*. 5.

7. Moore, Marianne. *The Poems of Marianne Moore*. Ed. Grace Schulman. London: Penguin, 2003. 239. Print.

8. Di Suvero, *Dreambook*, 266.

9. Judd, Donald. "Specific Objects." *Art in Theory 1900-2000: An Anthology of Changing Ideas*. Ed. Charles Harrison and Paul Wood. 2nd ed. Malden, MA: Blackwell Publishing, 2003. 827. Print.

10. Di Suvero, Mark. *Mark Di Suvero at Storm King Art Center*, 24.

11. Di Suvero, Mark. *Mark Di Suvero at Storm King Art Center*, 30.

12. Di Suvero, Mark. *Mark Di Suvero at Storm King Art Center*, 82.

13. Di Suvero, Mark. *Mark Di Suvero at Storm King Art Center*, 42.

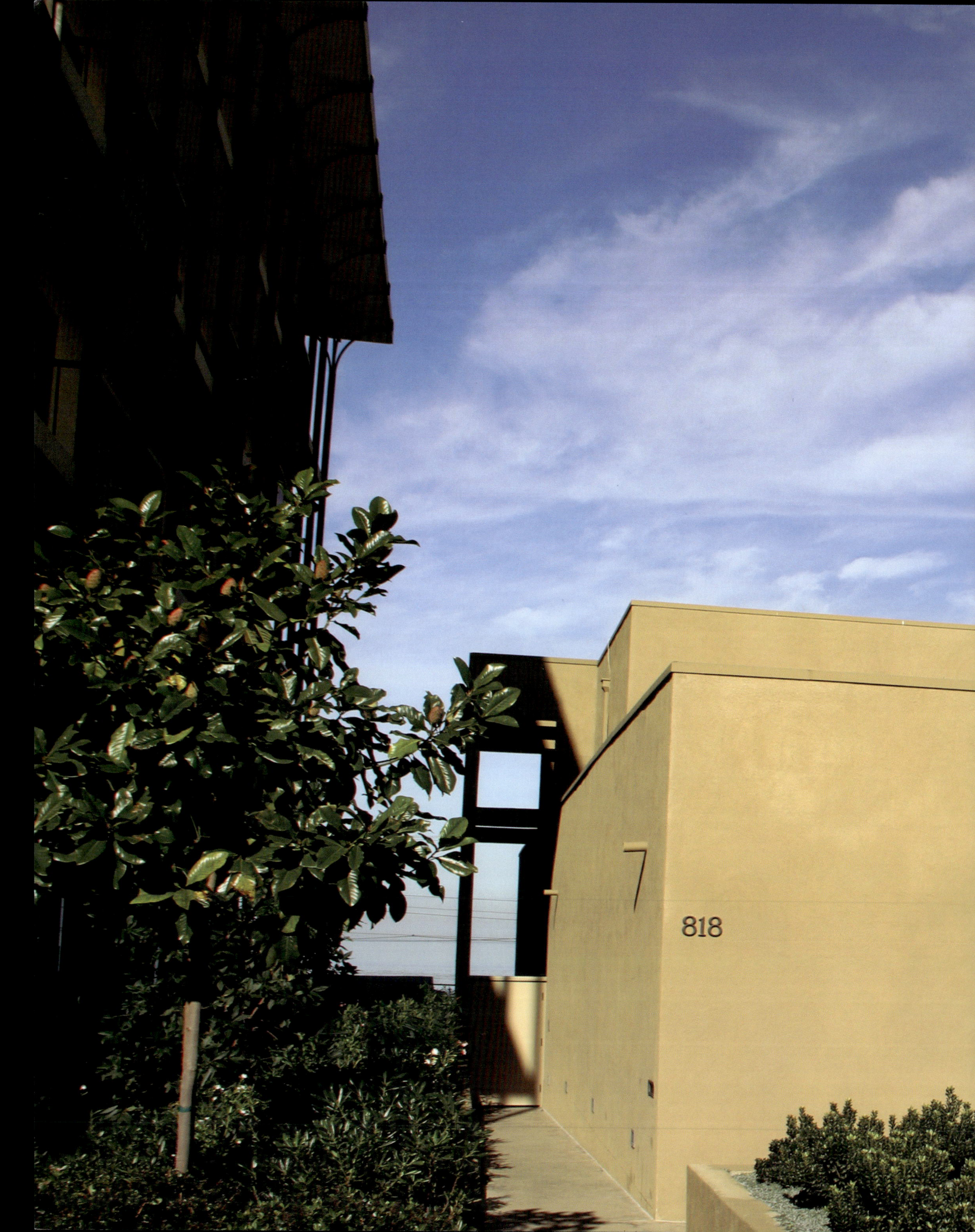
818

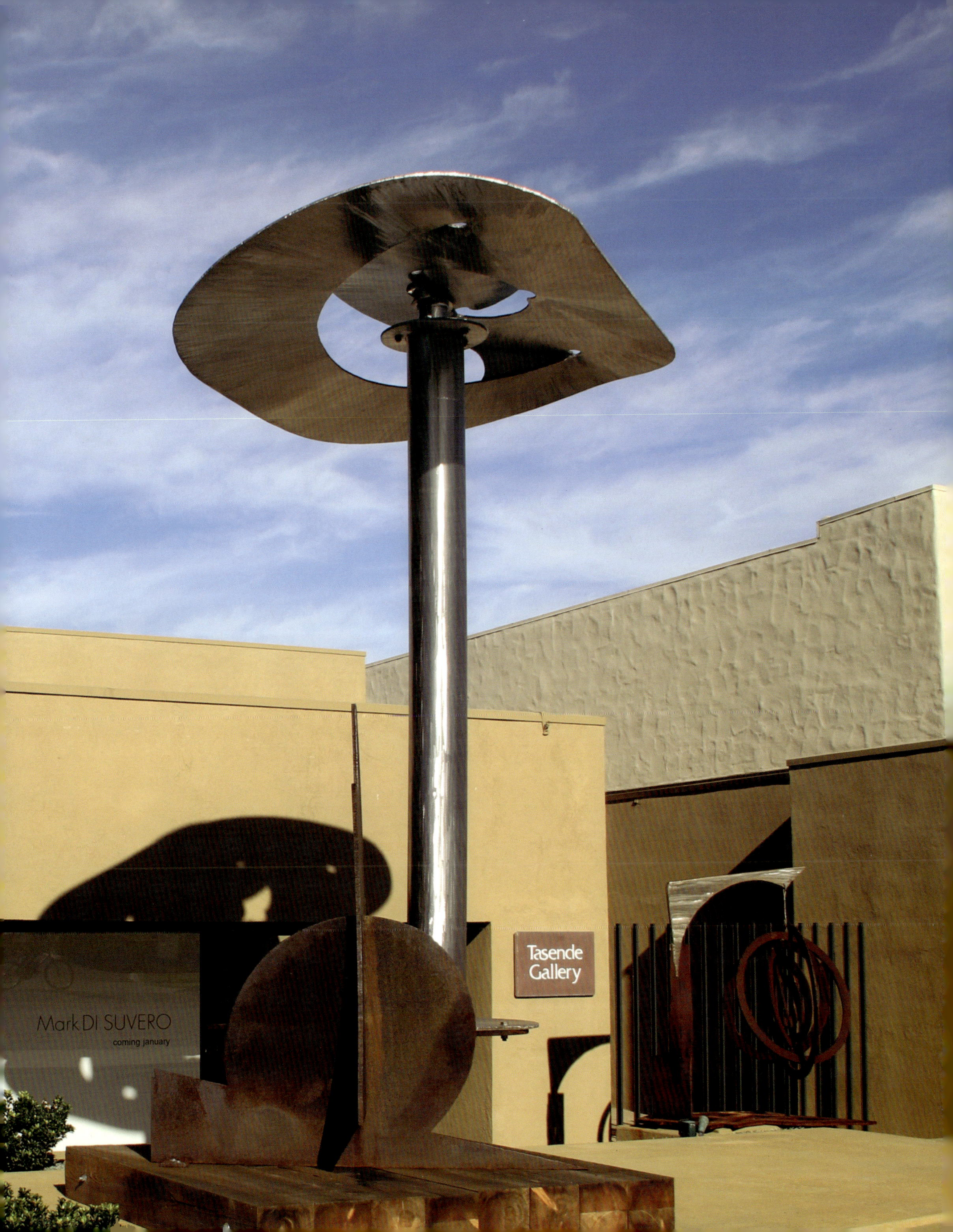
Mark DI SUVERO
coming january
Tasende
Gallery

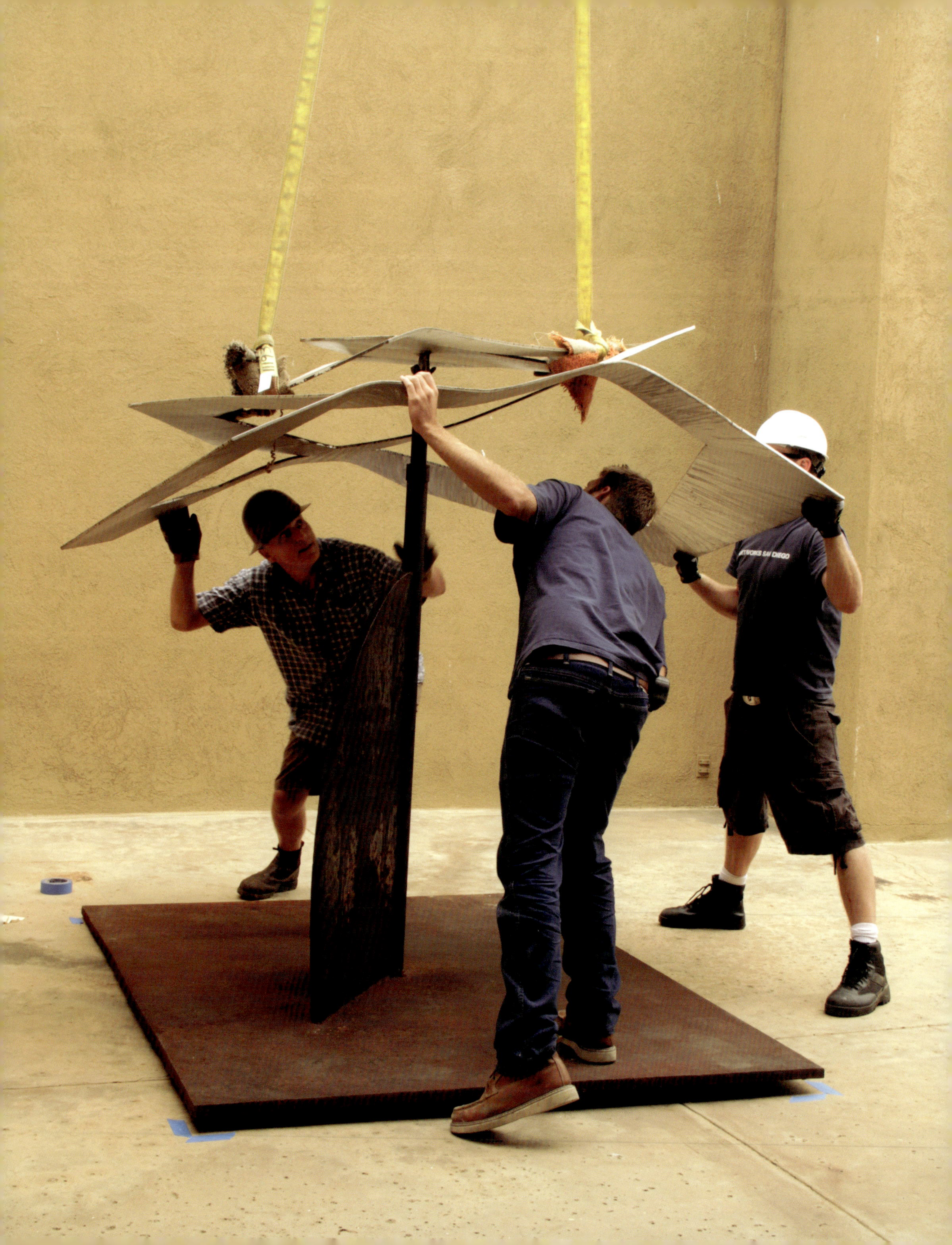

^{the} exhibition

Potluck I

2004, Stainless steel, 33 1/2 x 19 x 16 inches

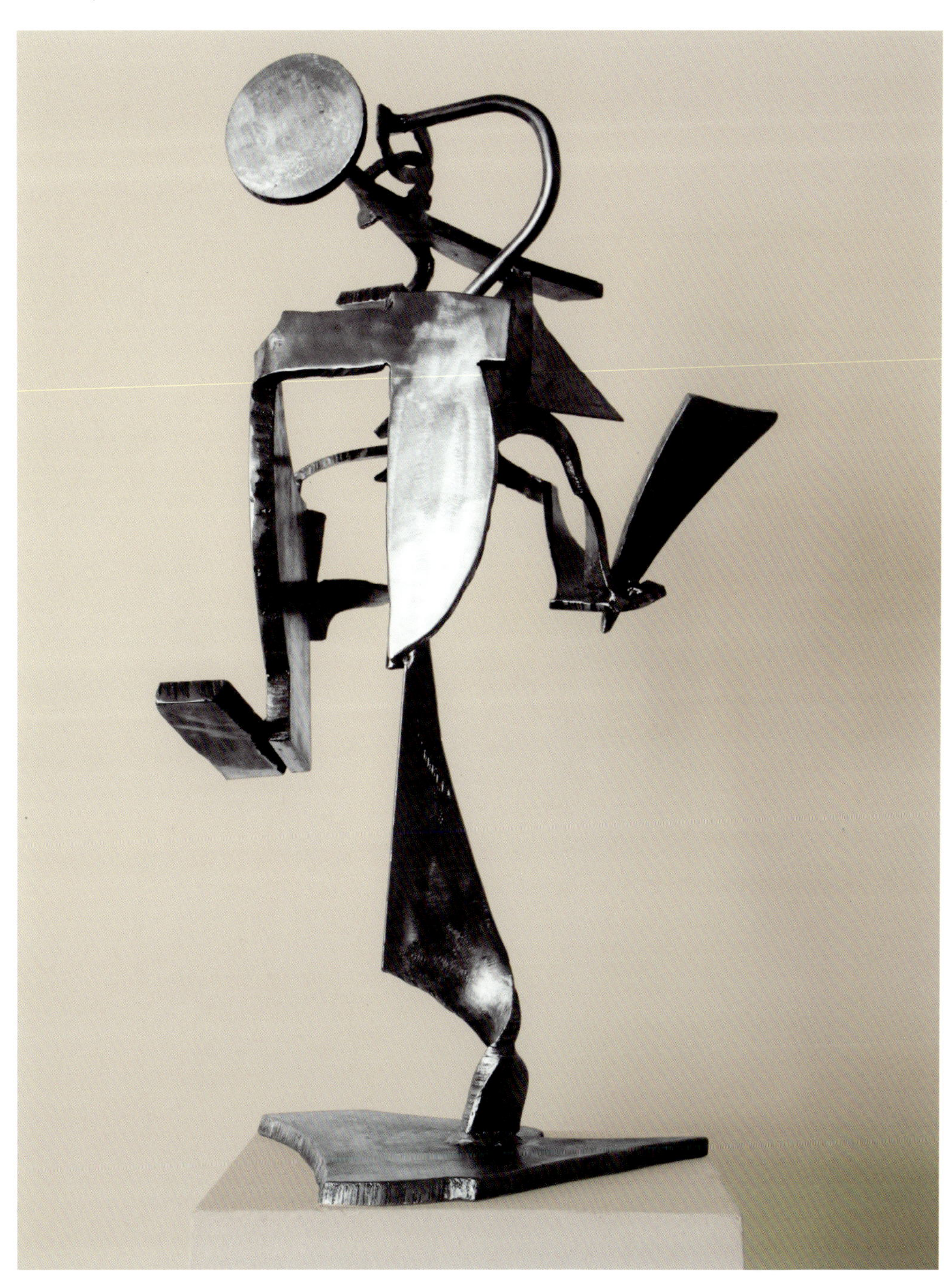

Arch Spirit

2003, Stainless steel and steel, 27 x 22 x 47 inches

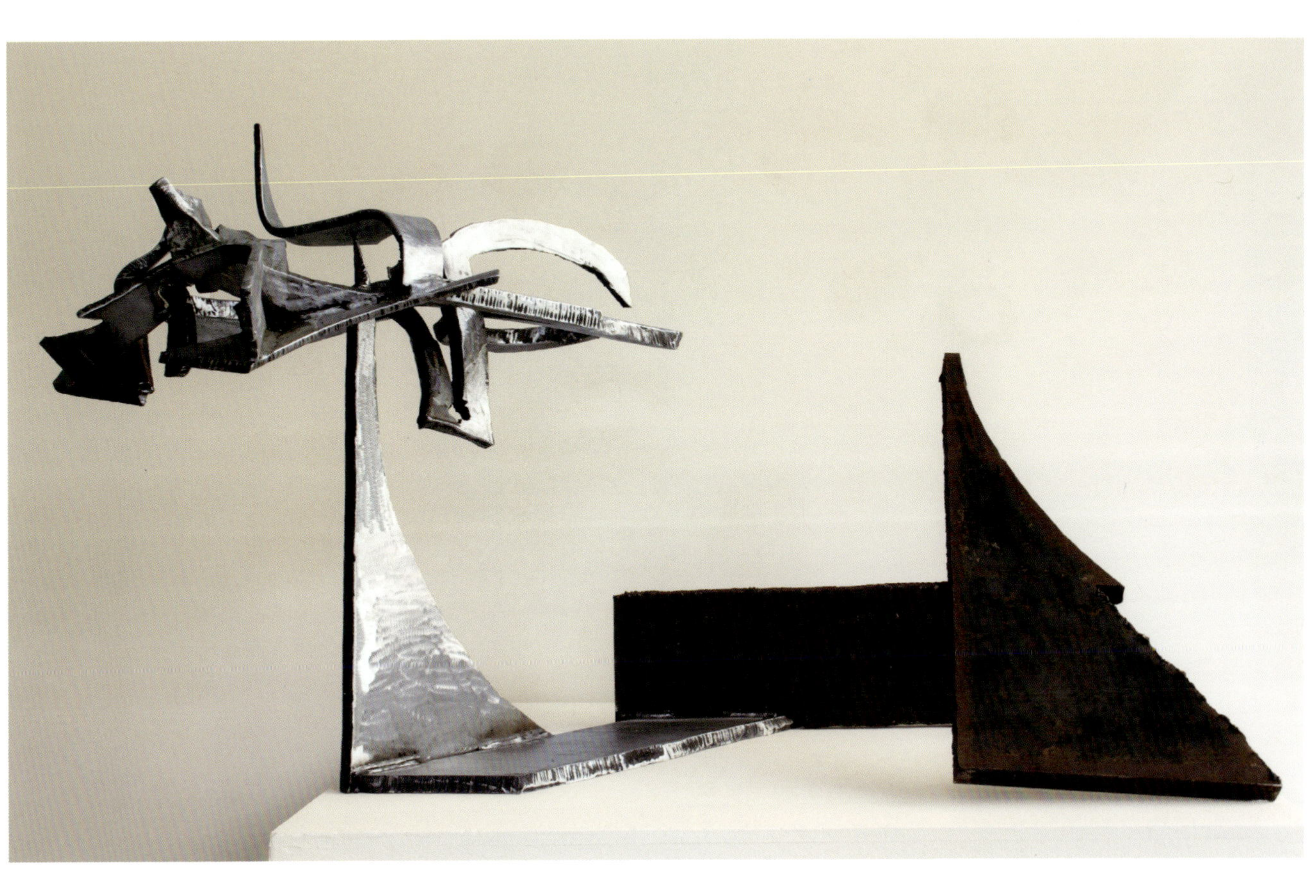

Nextro

2003, Stainless steel and steel, 57 x 73 x 36 inches

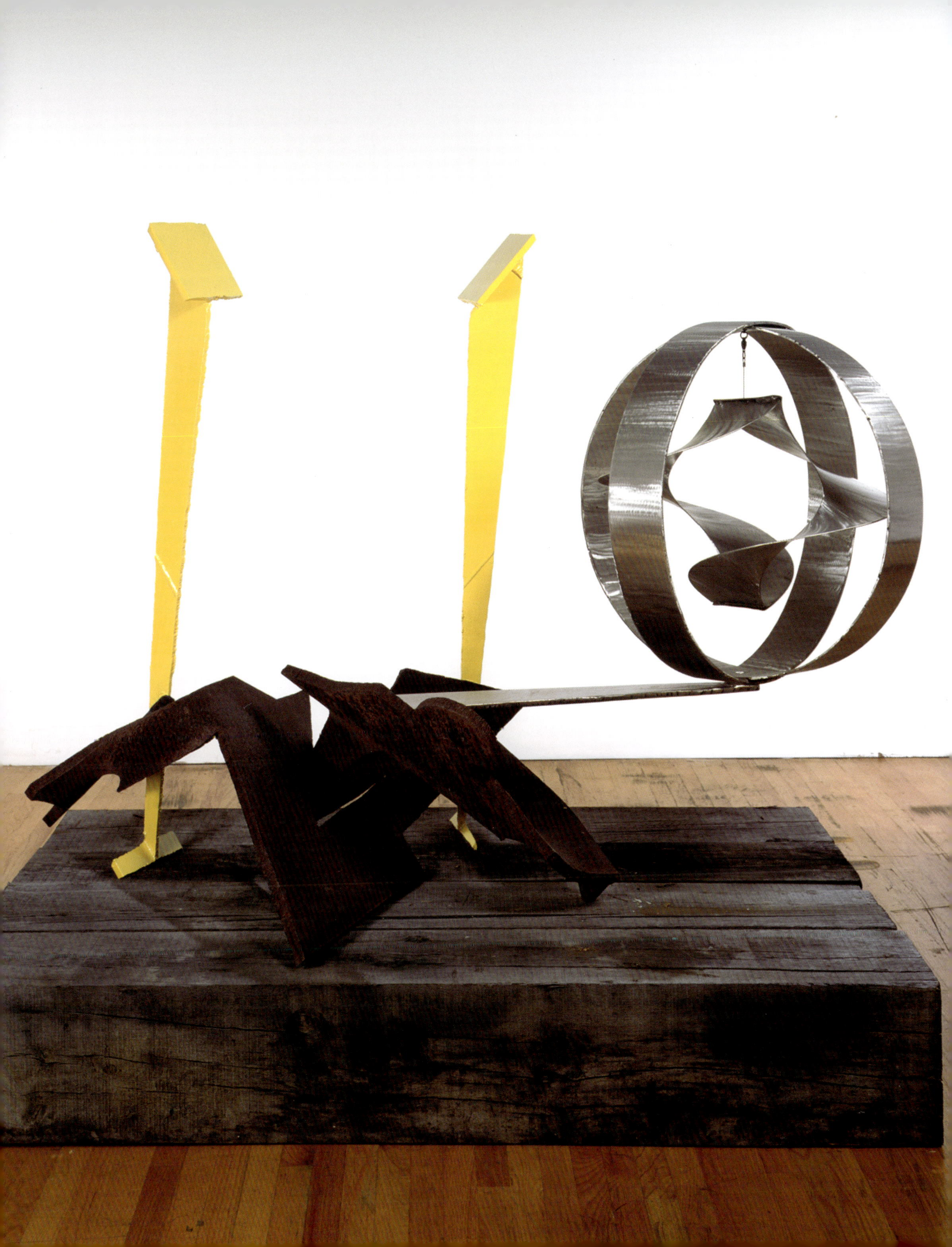

Morfygon

2002, Stainless steel and steel, 76 x 82 x 64 inches

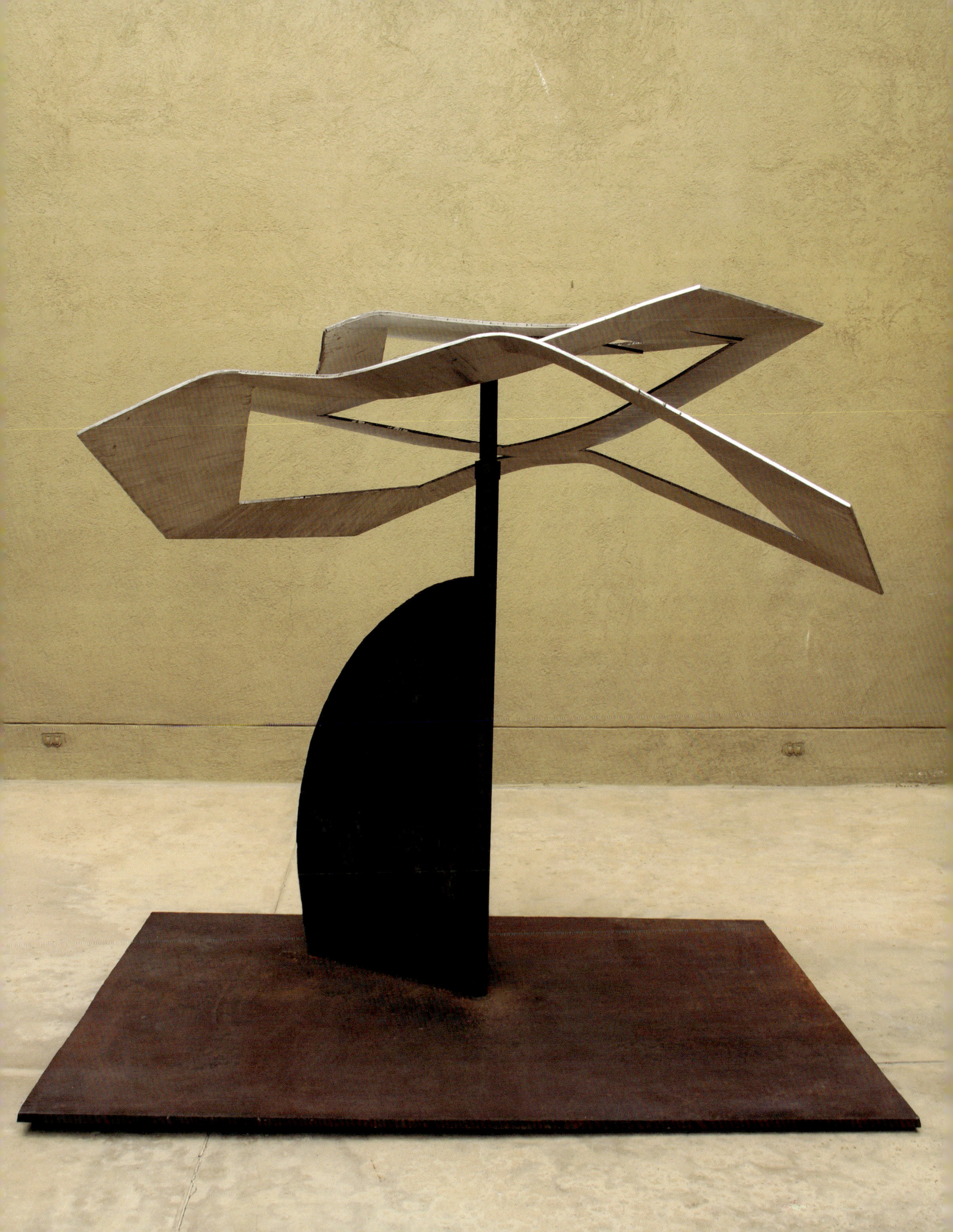

Untitled

2008, Corten and stainless steel, 83 1/2 x 57 x 60 inches

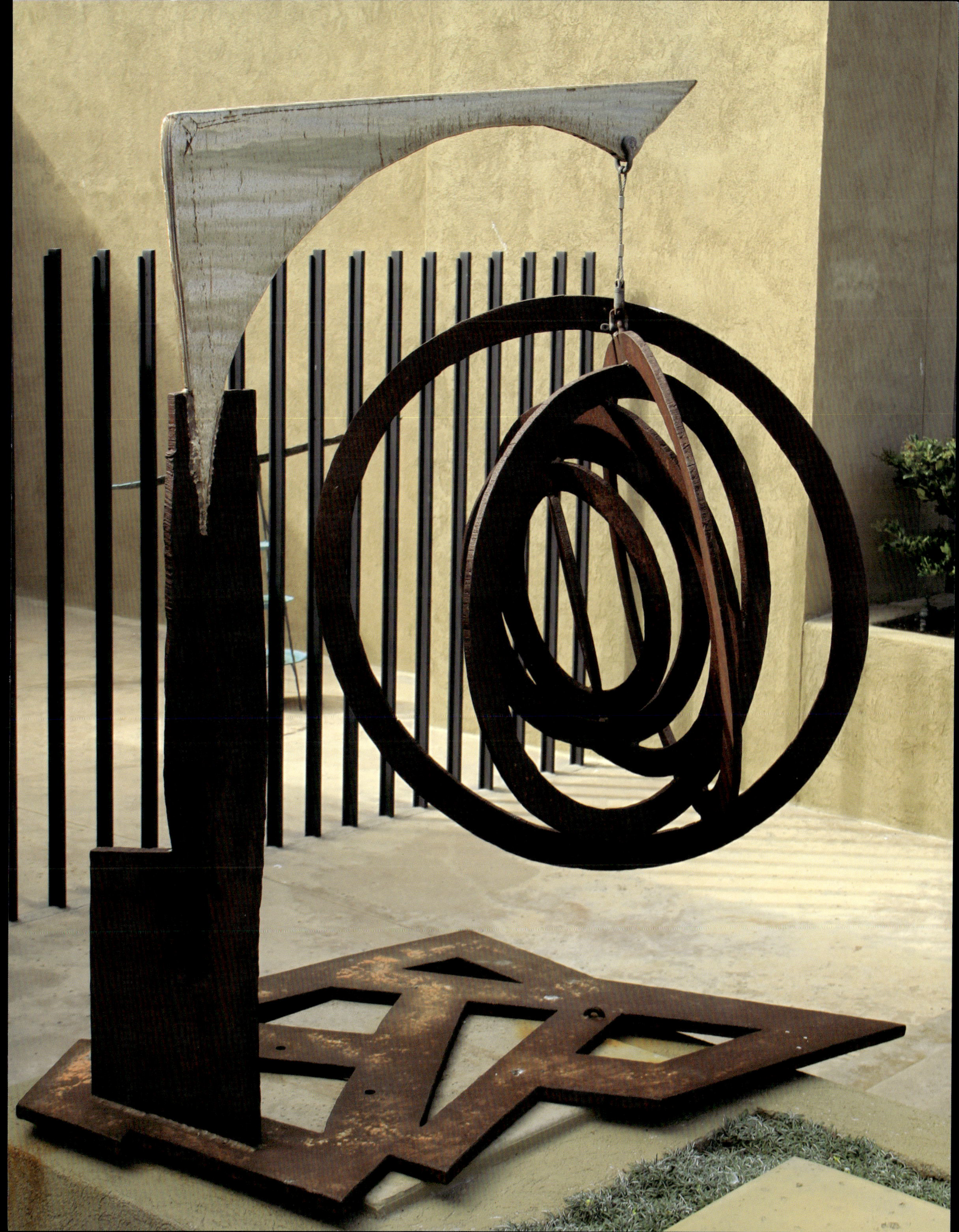

Ave Delirio

2001, Stainless steel and steel, 17'4" x 13' x 7'6"

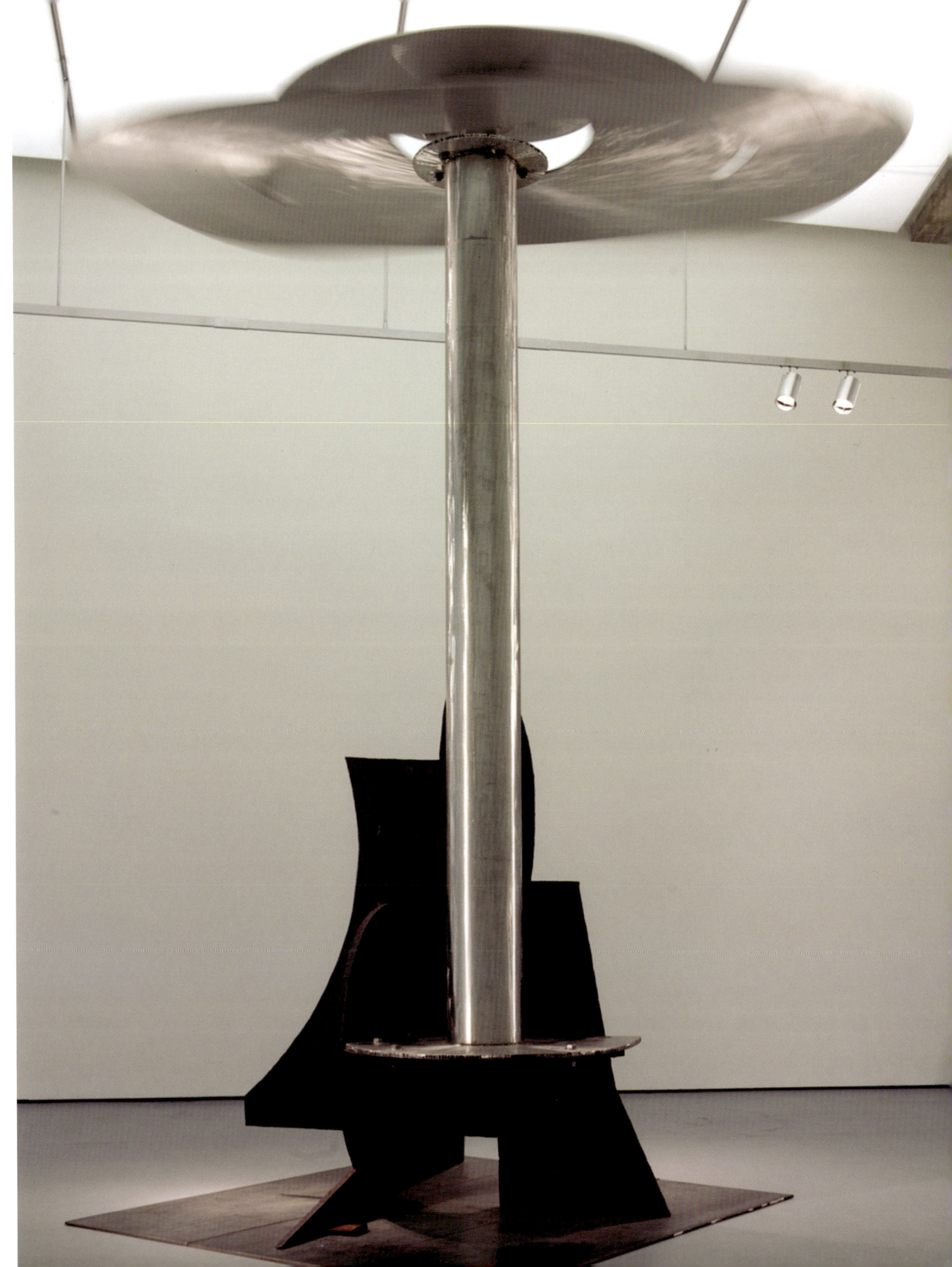

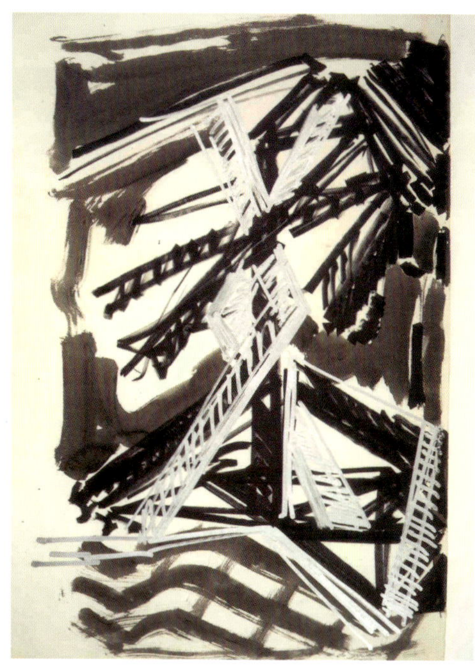

Untitled, 1983
Gouache and felt pens
35½ x 24¾ inches

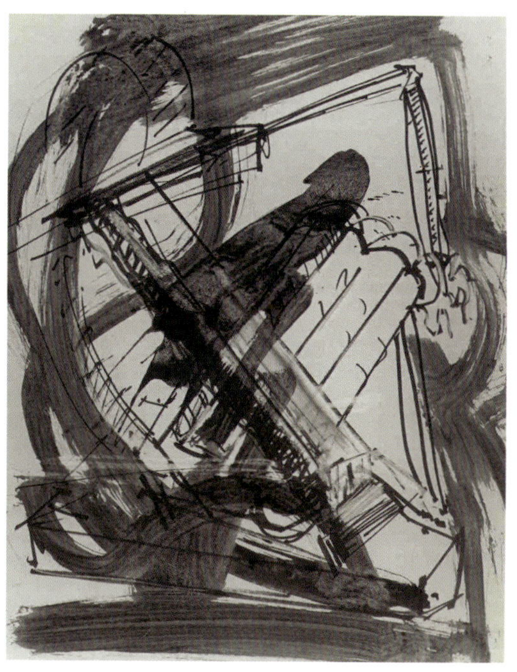

Untitled, 1968
Ink, pen and chalk
23¾ x 17¾ inches

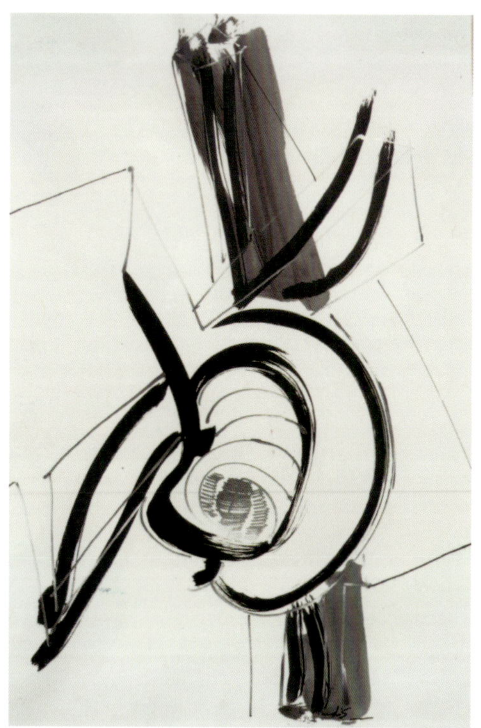

Untitled, 1990
Ink and aluminum paint
40 x 26 inches

Untitled, 1950
Pen and ink on paper
13¾ x 16¾ inches

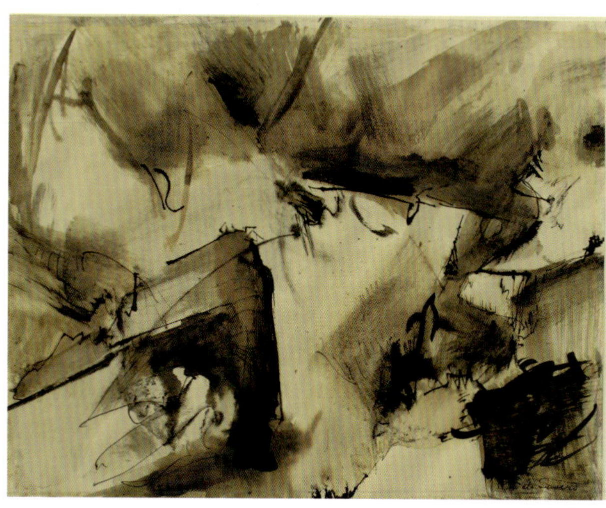

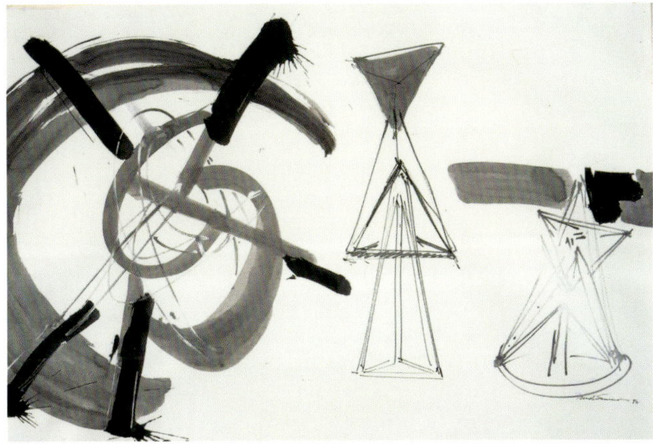

Untitled, 1990
Ink and aluminum paint
25 ¾ x 36 ¾ inches

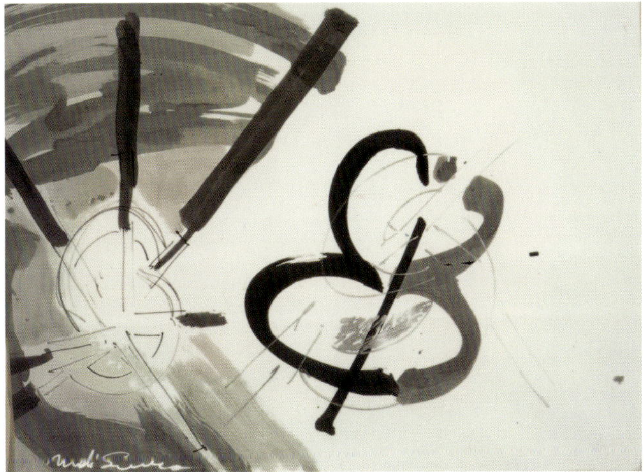

Untitled, 1990
Ink and aluminum paint
25 ¾ x 33 inches

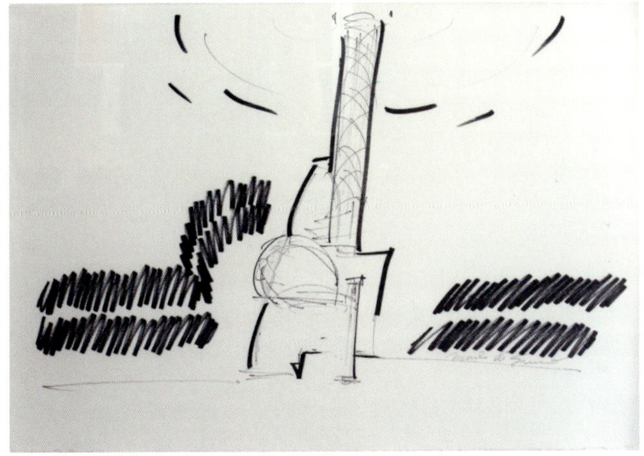

Untitled, date unknown
Felt pen on paper
22 x 30 inches

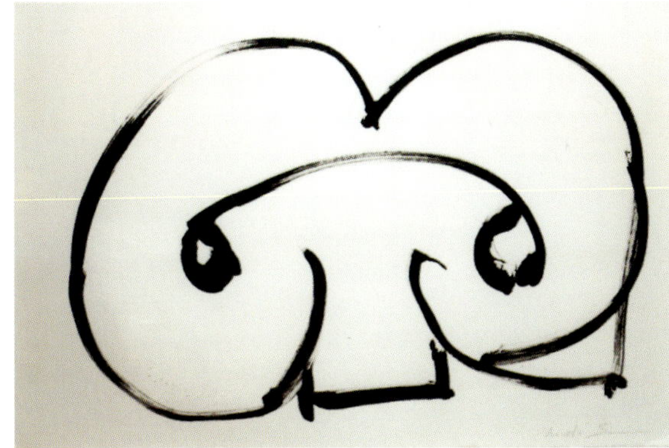

Untitled, c. 2001
Ink on paper
22 x 30 inches

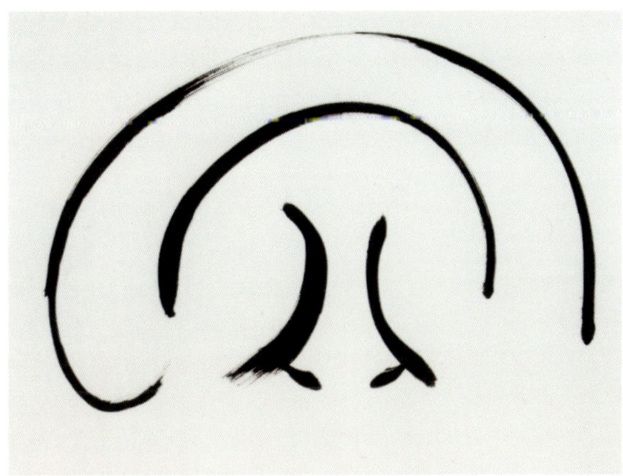

Untitled, date unknown
Ink on paper
22 x 30 inches

Mark di Suvero

1933	Born Shanghai, China
1941	Immigrated to United States
1953-54	San Francisco City College
1954-55	University of California, Santa Barbara
1956	University of California, Berkeley, B.A. Philosophy

solo exhibitions

1960	The Green Gallery, New York
1964	Park Place Gallery, New York
1965	Dwan Gallery, Los Angeles
1966	Park Place Gallery, New York
1967	Park Place Gallery, New York
1968	Lo Giudice Gallery, Chicago
1972	Van Abbemuseum, Eindhoven and City of Eindhoven, The Netherlands
	Wilhelm Lehmbruck Museum, Duisburg, Germany
	City of Chalon-sur-Saône, France (in cooperation with Centre National de Recherche, d'Animation et de Création pour les Arts Plastiques, Le Creusot, France, 1972-74)
1975	Jardin des Tuileries, Paris
	Whitney Museum of American Art, New York
1979	ConStruct, Chicago
1980	Ace Gallery, Venice, California
1983	Oil & Steel Gallery, New York
	Esprit Park, San Francisco
1985	Oil & Steel Gallery, New York
	Storm King Art Center, Mountainville, New York
1986	Hill Gallery, Birmingham, Michigan
1987	Akira Ikeda Gallery, Tokyo
	Oil & Steel Gallery, Long Island City, New York
1988	Württembergischer Kunstverein, Stuttgart, Germany
1989	Oil & Steel Gallery, Long Island City, New York
1990	City of Valence, France
	Galerie de France, Paris
	LA Louver, Venice, California
1991	Oil & Steel Gallery, Long Island City, New York
	Musée d'Art Moderne et d'Art Contemporain, Nice and City of Nice, France
	Akira Ikeda Gallery, Tokyo
1992	Chalon-sur-Saône, France
	Galerie Heike Curtze, Vienna, Austria
	Verein für Heimatpflege, Viersen, Germany
1993	Centre d'Art Passerelle, Brest, France
	Gagosian Gallery, New York
	Rettig y Martinez Gallery, Santa Fe, New Mexico
	Esprit Park, John Berggruen Gallery, San Francisco
1994	John Berggruen Gallery, San Francisco
	Institut Valencià d'Art Modern (IVAM), Centre Julio Gonzalez, Valencià, Spain
1995	46th Esposizione Internazionale d'Arte, la Biennale di Venezia, Italy
	Gagosian Gallery, New York
	Storm King Art Center, Mountainville, New York (1995- 96)
	Oil & Steel Gallery, Long Island City, New York
1996	Sheldon Art Museum, Lincoln, Nebraska
	Hill Gallery, Birmingham, Michigan
	Weigand Gallery, Belmont, California
	Galerie Jeanne-Bucher, Paris, France

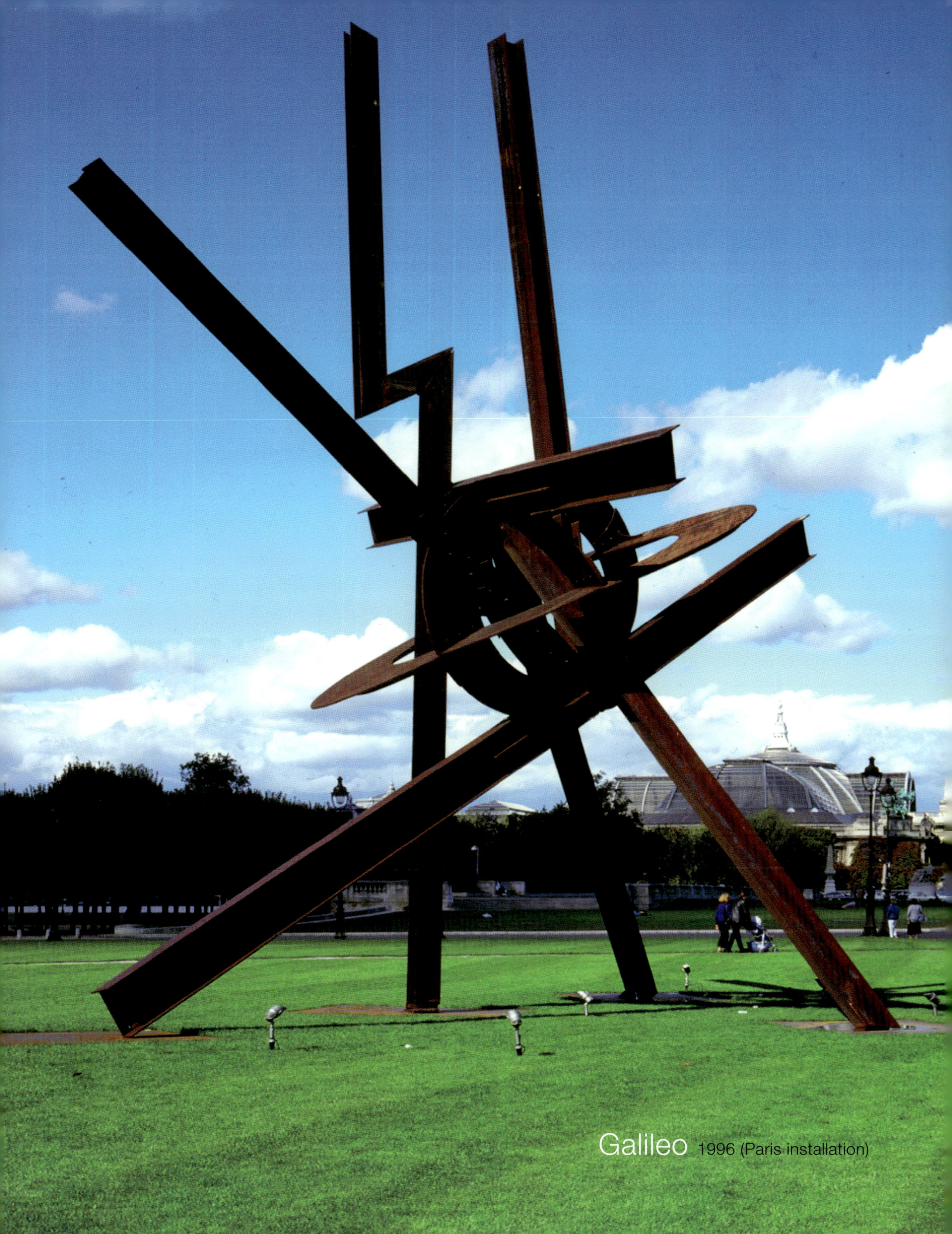

Galileo 1996 (Paris installation)

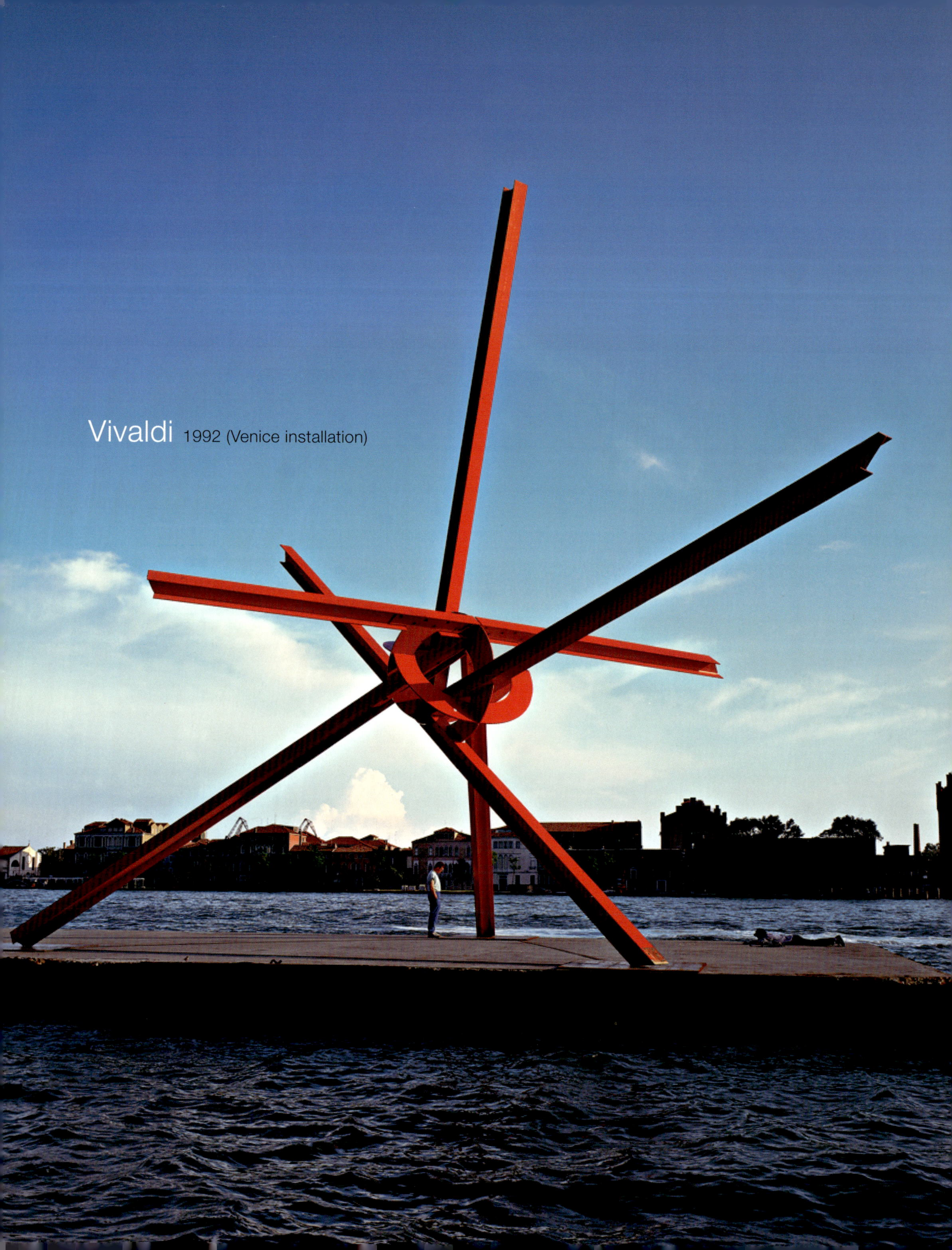
Vivaldi 1992 (Venice installation)

1997	Gagosian Gallery, New York
	City of Paris, France
1998	Orange County Museum of Art, Newport Beach, California
	Mark Moore Gallery, Santa Monica, California
	The Hiroshima Museum of Contemporary Art, Japan
1999	John Berggruen Gallery, San Francisco
2000	Danese Gallery, New York
2001	Gagosian Gallery, New York
	LA Louver, Venice, California
2002	Paula Cooper Gallery, New York
2003	John Berggruen Gallery, San Francisco
	Laumeier Sculpture Park, Saint Louis
	Paula Cooper Gallery, New York
	Akira Ikeda Gallery, Berlin
2004	Albion, Michael Hue-Williams Fine Art Limited, London
	Yorkshire Sculpture Park, Yorkshire, England
	Madison Square Park, New York
	Frederik Meijer Gardens & Sculpture Park, Grand Rapids, Michigan
2005	Storm King Art Center, Mountainville, New York (2005-06)
	Knoedler & Company, New York; in collaboration with Paula Cooper Gallery
2006	Paula Cooper Gallery, New York
2007	Millennium Park, Chicago
	Chicago Cultural Center, Chicago
	Paula Cooper Gallery, New York
	Akira Ikeda Gallery, Berlin
	City of Valenciennes, and the City of Cambrai, France (organized by Galerie Bruno Mory)
2008	LA Louver Gallery, Venice, California
	Paula Cooper Gallery, New York
	Fairchild Tropical Botanic Garden, Coral Gables, Florida
2009	John Berggruen Gallery, San Francisco
	Zane Bennett Contemporary Art, Santa Fe
	Paula Cooper Gallery, New York
2010	Paula Cooper Gallery, New York
	Morgan Library & Museum, New York
2011	Tasende Gallery, La Jolla, California

selected group exhibitions

1959	March Gallery, New York
1961	The Green Gallery, New York
1962	The Green Gallery, New York
	Continuity and Change, The Wadsworth Atheneum, Hartford, Connecticut
1963	*66th Annual American Exhibition: Directions in Contemporary Painting and Sculpture*, The Art Institute of Chicago
	Park Place Gallery, New York
1964	*Recent American Sculpture*, The Jewish Museum, New York
	Park Place Gallery, New York
1965	*Contemporary American Sculpture*, Musée Rodin, Paris
	The Green Gallery, New York
	Park Place Gallery, New York
1966	*Contemporary American Sculpture Section I*, assembled by the Howard and Jean Lipman Foundation and the Whitney Museum of American Art, New York; traveled in New York State
	Art of the United States: 1670 - 1966, Whitney Museum of American Art, New York
	Annual Exhibition 1966: Contemporary American Sculpture and Prints, Whitney Museum of American Art, New York
	Park Place Gallery, New York
	Toronto Symposium, Canada

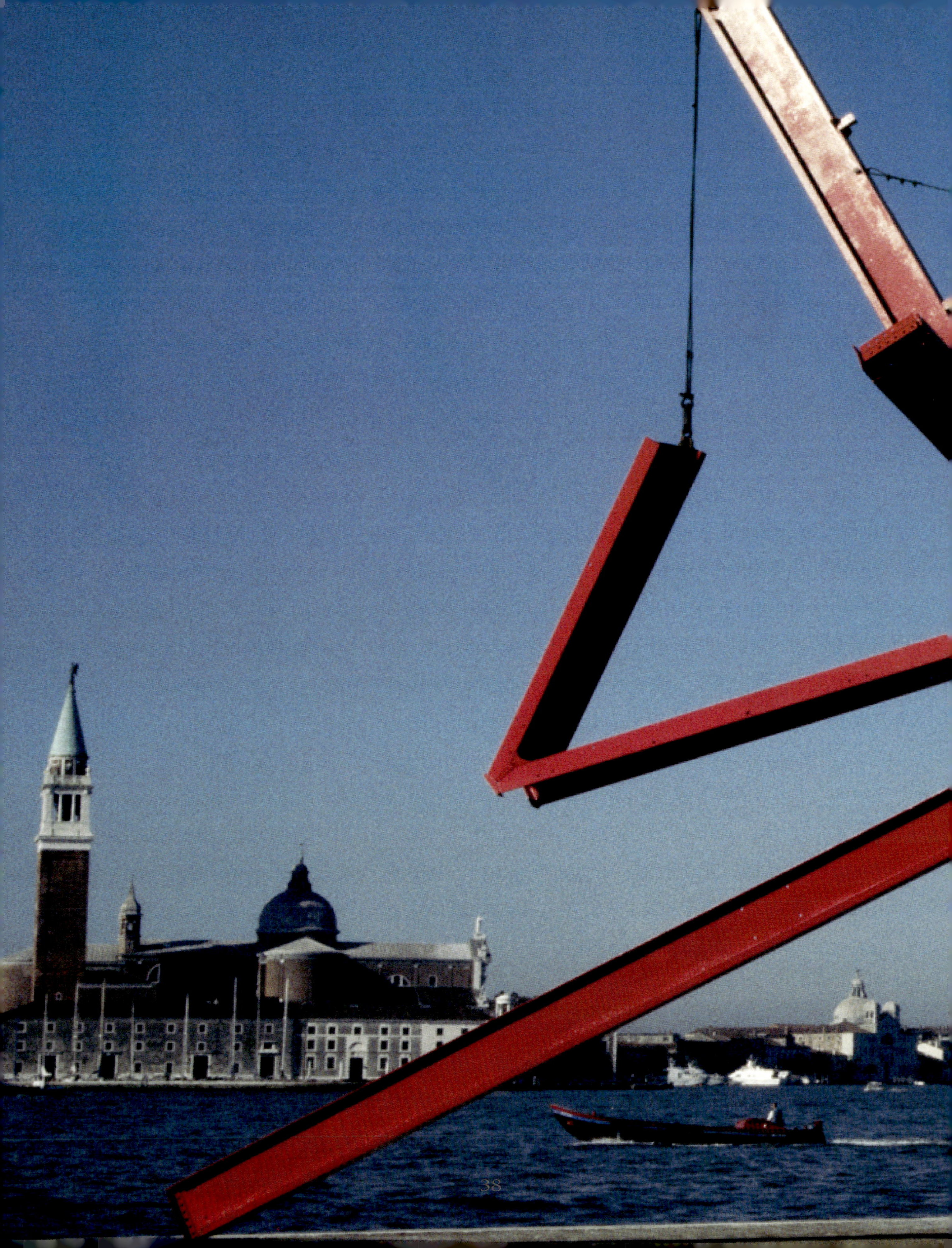

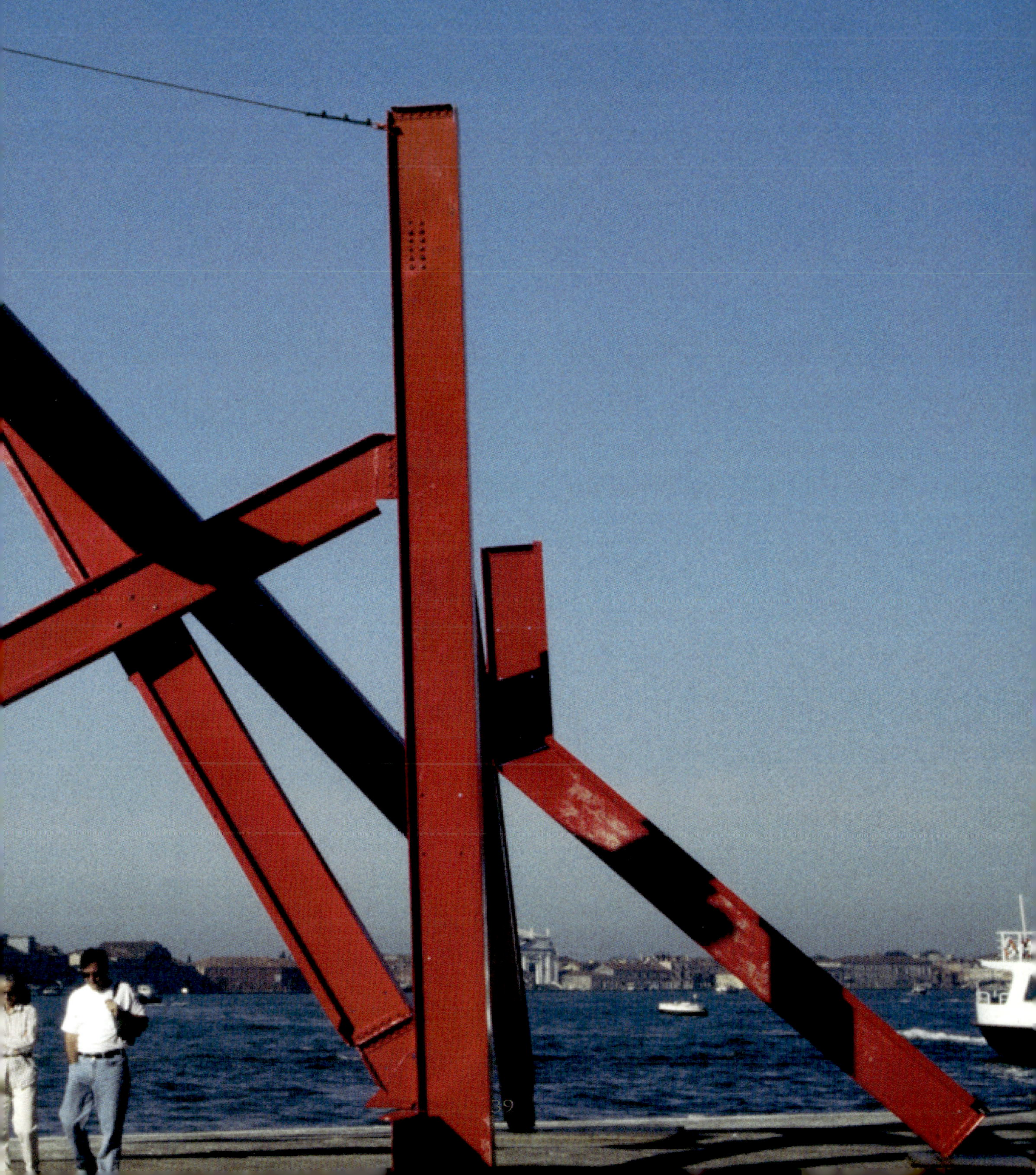

Are Years What?(For Marianne Moore) 1967 (Venice installation)

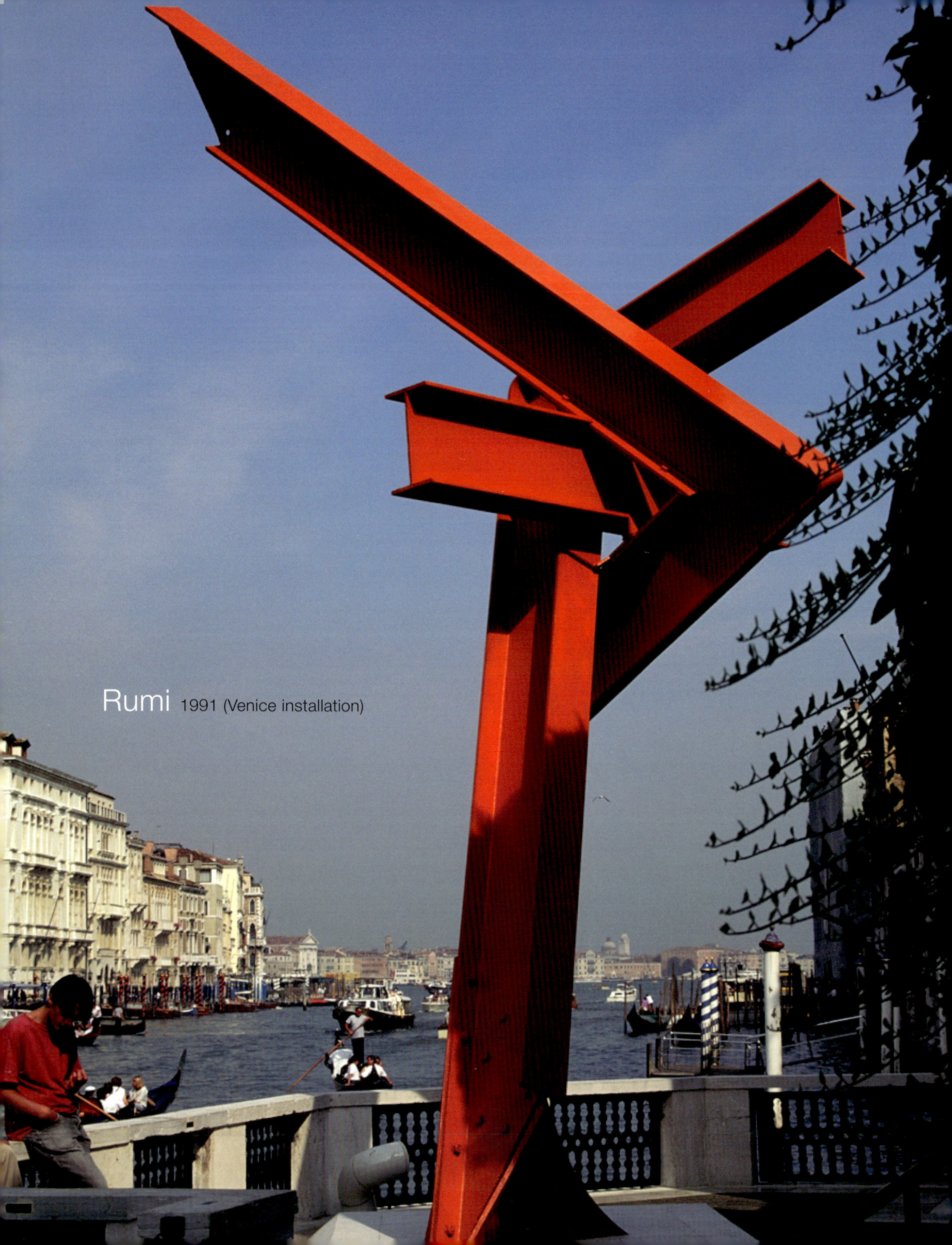
Rumi 1991 (Venice installation)

1967   *Sculpture International*, Solomon R. Guggenheim Museum, New York
          American Sculpture of the Sixties, Los Angeles County Museum of Art, Los Angeles
          7 for 67: Works by Contemporary American Sculptors, Saint Louis Art Museum
          Park Place Gallery, New York
1968   *Annual Exhibition: Contemporary American Sculpture*, Whitney Museum of American Art, New York
          Plus by Minus, Albright-Knox Art Gallery, Buffalo, New York
          Walter de Maria/ Mark di Suvero/ Richard Serra, Noah Goldowsky Gallery, New York
          Documenta IV, Kassel, Germany
          Martin Luther King Benefit, The Museum of Modern Art, New York
1969   *New York Painting and Sculpture: 1940 - 1970*, The Metropolitan Museum of Art, New York
1970   *Monumental Art*, The Contemporary Arts Center, Cincinnati, Ohio
          Noah Goldowsky Gallery, New York
1970   *Annual Exhibition: Contemporary American Sculpture*, Whitney Museum of American Art, New York
1971   *Works for New Spaces*, Walker Art Center, Minneapolis, Minnesota
          11th Biennale, Middelheim Sculpture Garden, Antwerp, Belgium
1972   *Art in Space*, Detroit Institute of Arts, Michigan
          Sculpture Off the Pedestal, Grand Rapids Art Museum, Grand Rapids, Michigan
          American Art—3rd Quarter Century, Seattle Art Museum, Washington
1973   *American Drawings 1963 - 1973*, Whitney Museum of American Art, New York
          Internationale Gartenbausstellung, Hamburg, Germany
          New York Collection for Stockholm, Moderna Museet, Stockholm
          A Selection of Recent Drawings, Noah Goldowsky Gallery, New York
1974   *Sculpture in the Park*, Grant Park, Chicago
          Public Sculpture/Urban Environment, The Oakland Museum, California
          Drawings: Studies for Unrealized Work for the University of Nevada,
               University Art Gallery, University of Nevada, Las Vegas
          The Condition of Sculpture, Hayward Gallery, London
1975   *Artists Make Toys*, Institute for Contemporary Art and Urban Resources,
               The Clocktower Gallery, New York
          Monumental Sculpture, Janie C. Lee Gallery, Houston
1976   *Biennale* of Sydney, Australia
          California Painting and Sculpture: The Modern Era, San Francisco Museum of Modern Art
1977   *Projects/New Urban Monuments*, Akron Art Institute, Akron, Ohio
          California Collections, San Francisco Museum of Modern Art
1978   *Inaugural Exhibition of the Wave Hill Sculpture Garden*, Bronx, New York
          New York: The State of Art, New York State Museum, Albany, New York
          California: 3 By 8 Twice, Honolulu Academy of Arts
          Group Show, ConStruct, Chicago
          Janie C. Lee Gallery, Houston
1979   *On Sculpture*, Neuberger Museum, State University of New York, Purchase, New York
          The Prospect Mountain Sculpture Show, Lake George Arts Project, Lake George, New York
1980   *Homage to Picasso*, Walker Art Center, Minneapolis, Minnesota
          American Sculpture: Gifts of Howard and Jean Lipman, Whitney Museum of American Art, New York
          Ten Abstract Sculptures, American & European 1940-1980, Max Hutchison Gallery, New York
          Urban Encounters: Art, Architecture, Audience, Institute of Contemporary Art, Philadelphia
1981   *Contemporary Painting/ Sculpture I*, Oil & Steel Gallery, New York
1982   *Contemporary Painting/Sculpture II + III*, Oil & Steel Gallery, New York
          20 American Artists: Sculpture 1982, San Francisco Museum of Modern Art
1983   *Sculpture: The Tradition in Steel*, Nassau County Museum of Art, Roslyn Harbor, New York
          The First Show: Painting and Sculpture from Eight Collections, 1940-1980,
               The Museum of Contemporary Art, Los Angeles
1984   *Contemporary Painting and Sculpture: 1957-1984*, Oil & Steel Gallery, New York
          Painting and Sculpture, Hill Gallery, Birmingham, Michigan
1985   *Sense and Sensibility*, Hill Gallery, Birmingham, Michigan
          Ontogeny: Sculpture and Painting by 20th Century American Sculptors, New York
          Studio School of Drawing, Painting, and Sculpture, New York

1986
International Exhibition VII, Solomon R. Guggenheim Museum, New York
The Third Dimension: Sculpture of the New York School, Whitney Museum of American Art, New York
Oil & Steel Gallery, Long Island City, New York
An American Renaissance: Painting and Sculpture Since 1940,
     Museum of Art, Fort Lauderdale, Florida
American Academy of Arts and Letters, New York
Selected Works of 20th Century Masters, John Berggruen Gallery, San Francisco
Indoor/Outdoor Sculpture Exhibition, El Bohio Community and Cultural Center, New York
The Second Newport Biennial: The Bay Area,
     Newport Harbor Art Museum, Newport Beach, California
Inaugural Exhibition, Socrates Sculpture Park, Long Island City, New York
Sculpture, Hill Gallery, Birmingham, Michigan
Individuals: A Selected History of Contemporary Art, 1945-1986,
     The Museum of Contemporary Art, Los Angeles

1987
Oil & Steel Gallery, Long Island City, New York
Sculpture: Walk On/Sit Down/Go Through, Socrates Sculpture Park, Long Island City, New York
Outside In: Socrates Sculpture Park, City Gallery at Columbus Circle, New York
Aspects of Collage, Assemblage and the Found Object in the 20th Century,
     Solomon R. Guggenheim Museum, New York
Oil & Steel Gallery, Long Island City, New York

1988
Selected Sculpture, John Berggruen Gallery, San Francisco
Sculpture Since the Sixties from the Permanent Collection of the Whitney Museum of American Art,
     Whitney Museum of American Art at Equitable Center, New York

1989
Oil & Steel Gallery, Long Island City, New York
10th Anniversary Exhibition, Tasende Gallery, La Jolla, California
The "Junk" Aesthetic: Assemblage of the 1950s and Early 1960s,
     Whitney Museum of American Art at Equitable Center, New York
A Decade of American Drawing, Daniel Weinberg Gallery, Los Angeles
Sculptors Working, Socrates Sculpture Park, Long Island City, New York

1990
Sculpture City, Socrates Sculpture Park, Long Island City, New York
Sculpture, Gagosian Gallery, New York
Group Exhibition, Manny Silverman Gallery, Los Angeles

1991
Grass Roots Art Energy, Socrates Sculpture Park, Long Island City, New York

1992
Grass Roots Art Energy, Socrates Sculpture Park, Long Island City, New York
Akira Ikeda Gallery, Taura, Japan
Hill Gallery, Birmingham, Michigan
Table Sculpture by Modern and Contemporary Masters, Andre Emmerich Gallery, New York
Winter's Edge, Okun Gallery, Santa Fe, New Mexico

1993
Full Life, Socrates Sculpture Park, Long Island City, New York
The Second Dimension: Twentieth Century Sculptor's Drawings from the Brooklyn Museum,
     The Brooklyn Museum
University Art Museum, University of New Mexico, Albuquerque

1994
Le Temps d'un Dessin, Galerie de l'Ecole des Beaux Arts de Lorient, France
Spring Equinox Exhibition, Tasende Gallery, La Jolla, California
International 93-94, Socrates Sculpture Park, Long Island City, New York
Self Portrait, David Rettig Fine Arts, Inc., Santa Fe, New Mexico
New Sculpture, LA Louver, Venice, California
The Essential Gesture, Newport Harbor Art Museum, Newport Beach, California
Another Dimension: Paintings by Sculptors, John Weber Gallery, New York

1995
T Curtsnoc Fine Arts, Miami, Florida
Socrates Sculpture Park, Long Island City, New York
John Berggruen Gallery, San Francisco
LA Louver, Venice, California
Hill Gallery, Birmingham, Michigan
Twentieth Century American Sculpture II, The White House, Washington, D.C.
Environmental Sculptures, Kukje Gallery, Seoul, South Korea

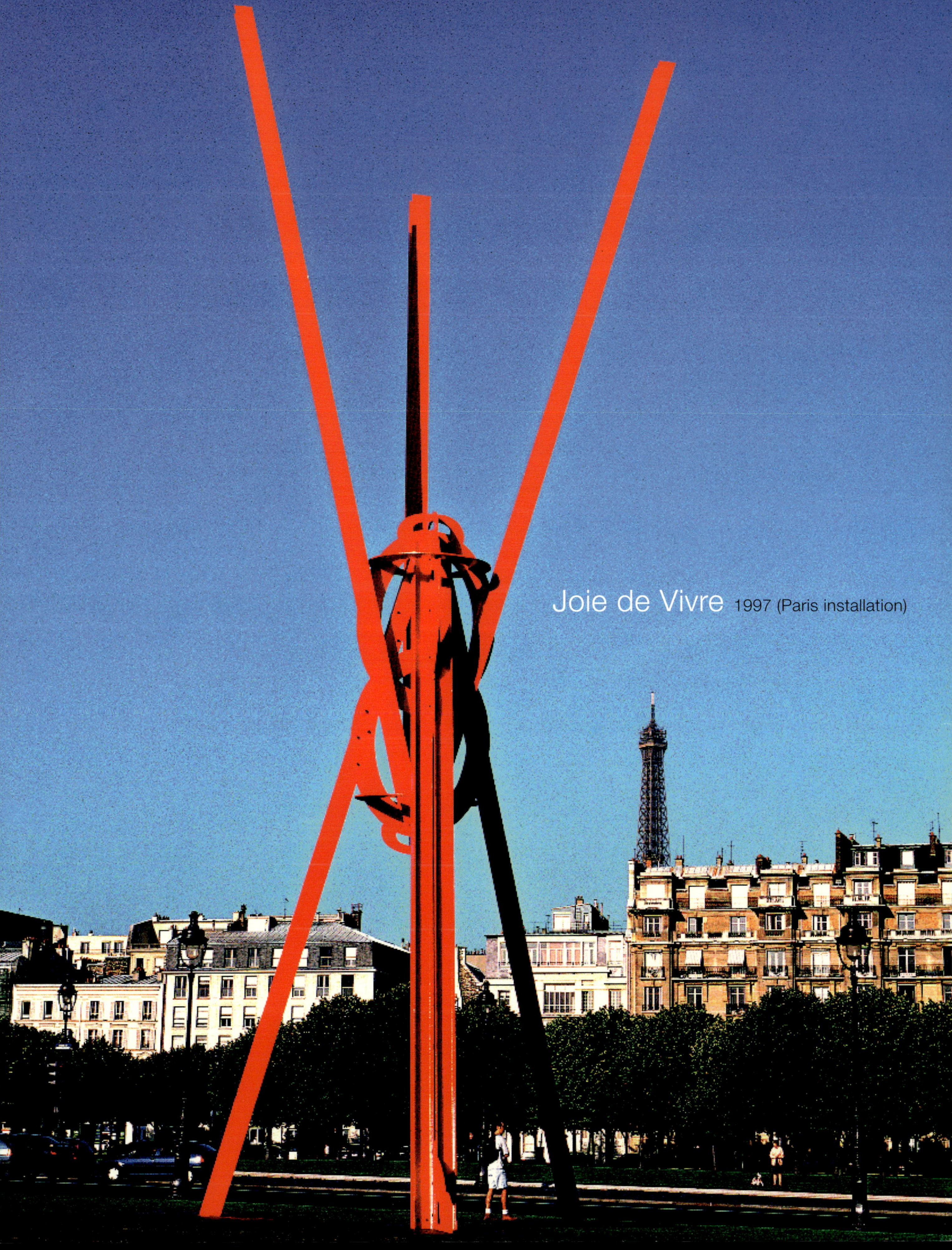
Joie de Vivre 1997 (Paris installation)

1996	T Curtsnoc Fine Arts, Miami, Florida
	Tenth Anniversary Season, Socrates Sculpture Park, Long Island City, New York
	San Francisco Museum of Modern Art
	The Human Body in Contemporary American Sculpture, Gagosian Gallery, New York
	The Philip Johnson Collection, The Museum of Modern Art, New York
	The Sculpture Garden @ 590 Madison Avenue, New York
	John Berggruen Gallery, San Francisco
	Isetan Museum of Art, Japan
	Franconia Sculpture Park, Shaffer, Michigan
	Masters of American Sculpture, Gagosian Gallery, New York
1997	*International 97*, Socrates Sculpture Park, Long Island City, New York
	Boom, T Curtsnoc Fine Arts, Miami, Florida
	John Berggruen Gallery, San Francisco
	Gagosian Gallery, New York
	Two Sculptors Gallery, New York
	The Nasher Collection, Solomon R. Guggenheim Museum, New York
	Queens Museum of Art, New York
1998	*Escape Velocity*, Socrates Sculpture Park, Long Island City, New York
	The Edward R. Broida Collection; A Selection of Works, Orlando Museum of Art, Florida
	100 Years of Sculpture: From the Pedestal to the Pixel, Walker Art Center, Minneapolis
1999	*Group Show*, Gagosian Gallery, New York
	Contemporary Abstraction, Klein Art Works, Chicago
	The American Century: Art and Culture 1900-2000, Whitney Museum of American Art, New York
	RE-STRUCTURE, Grinnell College Art Gallery, Grinnell, Iowa
2000	*Welded Sculpture in the Twentieth Century*, Neuberger Museum of Art, Purchase, New York
	Acquisitions, John Berggruen Gallery, San Francisco
	Renzo Piano, Centre Pompidou, Paris
2001	*Venice Art Walk*, Venice, California
	Mark di Suvero/Renzo Piano/Nasher Sculpture Center, Galerie Bruno Mory, Besanceuil, France
	Sculpture, Drawings and Works in Relief, John Berggruen Gallery, San Francisco
	Mark di Suvero, Ellsworth Kelly, Donald Judd, Sol Lewitt, Rudolph Stingel: Sculpture, Paula Cooper Gallery, New York
2002	*Oh Beautiful!: American Paintings, Drawings and Sculpture*, John Berggruen Gallery, San Francisco
2003	*Sculpture Monumentale*, Galerie Bruno Mory, Chateau de Fléchères, Fareins, France
	Intuition and Response: Masterworks from the Edward Broida Collection, Jacksonville Museum of Art, Florida
2004	*Moved*, Hunter College/Times Square Gallery, New York
	Sculpture, LA Louver, Venice, California
	Life Understood, Hill Gallery, Birmingham, Michigan
2005	*Sculpture Sonoma 2005*, Sonoma Valley Museum of Art, California
	Summer 2005, Manny Silverman Gallery, Los Angeles
	Highlights: New Acquisitions, John Berggruen Gallery, San Francisco
	Picturing America: Selections from the Whitney Museum of American Art, Nagasaki Prefectural Museum, Japan
2006	*Whitney Biennial 2006: Day for Night*, Whitney Museum of American Art, New York
	Richard Bellamy and Mark di Suvero 2005-2006, Storm King Art Center, Mountainville, New York
	Art Basel, Art Unlimited, Switzerland, Paula Cooper Gallery, New York; in conjunction with Gretchen Berggruen Gallery, San Francisco
	A Four Dimensional Being Writes Poetry On a Field With Sculptures: An Exhibition Curated by Charles Ray, Mathew Marks Gallery, New York
	Outdoor Sculpture, David Zwirner, New York
2007	*Not For Sale*, P.S.1 Contemporary Art Center, Queens, New York
	LIC, Socrates Sculpture Park, Long Island City, New York
2008	*FREEDOM*, The Hague, The Netherlands
	Reimagining Space: The Park Place Gallery Group in 1960s New York, Blanton Museum of Art, University of Texas, Austin

Molded, Folded, & Found, Greenberg Van Duren Gallery, New York
Summer in the City, John Berggruen Gallery, San Francisco

2009 *The Sculptor's Hand*, Tasende Gallery, La Jolla, California
Nueva York-El Papel de las Ultimas Vanguardias, El Museo de Arte Contemporáneo Esteban Vicente, Segovia, Spain
The Third Mind: American Artists Contemplate Asia, 1860-1989, Solomon R. Guggenheim Museum, New York
In Sight: Selections from the Collection, Laumeier Sculpture Park, St. Louis, Missouri
After Image, Paula Cooper Gallery, New York
Independent Visions, John Berggruen Gallery, San Francisco

2010 *Drawing on Sculpture*, University of Dallas Beatrice M. Haggerty Gallery, Texas
5+5: New Perspectives and The View from Here: Storm King at Fifty, Storm King Art Center, Mountainville, NY
International VSA Arts Festival, John F. Kennedy Center for the Performing Arts, Washington D.C.
Contemporary Sculptors Celebrate the Legacy of Frederick and Lena Meijer, Frederick Meijer Gardens & Sculpture Park, Grand Rapids, Michigan
Calder to Warhol: Introducing the Fischer Collection, San Francisco Museum of Modern Art, San Francisco
Summertime, Hill Gallery, Bloomfield Hills, Michigan

selected public collections

Akron Museum of Art, Ohio
The City of Baltimore
Baltimore Museum of Art
The Bradley Family Foundation Sculpture Garden, Milwaukee
The City of Chalon-sur-Saône, France
Cincinnati Art Museum, Ohio
Currier Museum of Art, Manchester, New Hampshire
Daimler Art Collection, Potsdamer Platz, Berlin
Dallas Museum of Art
Denver Art Museum
Des Moines Art Center
Detroit Institute of Arts
Fairmount Park Association, Philadelphia
Fine Arts Museums of San Francisco, Legion of Honor
Fort Wayne Museum of Art, Indiana
Frederik Meijer Gardens and Sculpture Park, Grand Rapids, Michigan
Hirshhorn Museum and Sculpture Garden, Smithsonian Institution, Washington, D.C.
Hood Museum of Art, Dartmouth College, Hanover, New Hampshire
Indianapolis Art Museum
Iris & B. Gerald Cantor Arts Center for Visual Arts at Stanford University, California
Kröller-Müller Museum, Otterlo, The Netherlands
Los Angeles County Museum of Art
Martin Z. Margulies Sculpture Park at Florida International University, Miami
The Menil Collection, Houston
Miami University Art Museum, Oxford, Ohio
Milwaukee Art Museum
Moderna Museet, Stockholm
Muhlenberg College, Allentown, Pennsylvania
Museum of Contemporary Art, Chicago
The Museum of Contemporary Art, Los Angeles
The Museum of Modern Art, New York
Nasher Sculpture Center, Dallas

Nathan Manilow Sculpture Park at Governors State University, University Park, Illinois
National Gallery of Art, Washington, D.C.
National Gallery of Australia, Canberra
The Nelson-Atkins Museum of Art, Kansas City, Missouri
Oakland Museum of California
Palm Springs Desert Museum, California
Saint Louis Art Museum, Missouri
The City and County of San Francisco, San Francisco Arts Commission
San Francisco Museum of Modern Art
Seattle Art Museum, Olympic Sculpture Park
Skulpturenpark Köln, Cologne
Storm King Art Center, Mountainville, New York
Technopôle Brest-Iroise, Brest, France
Toledo Museum of Art, Ohio
University of Iowa Museum of Art, Iowa City
University of Nebraska—Lincoln, Sheldon Memorial Art Gallery
The City of Valence, France
Walker Art Center, Minneapolis
Weatherspoon Art Museum at the University of North Carolina at Greensboro
Western Washington University, Bellingham
Whitney Museum of American Art, New York
Yale University Art Gallery, New Haven

selected bibliography

2008   di Suvero, Mark. *Mark di Suvero Dreambook.* Berkeley: University of California Press
2007   *Mark di Suvero*. Valenciennes, France: Galerie Bruno Mory
2006   Stern, Peter H., et al. *Richard Bellamy. Mark di Suvero*. Mountainville, New York:
                Storm King Art Center
2005   *Mark di Suvero: Indoors*. New York: Knoedler & Company
2004-05   *Mark di Suvero*. Grand Rapids, Michigan: Frederik Meijer Gardens & Sculpture Park
2004   *Mark di Suvero*. London, England: Albion, Michael Hue-Williams Fine Art Ltd.
2003-05   *Mark di Suvero: Dragons in the Sky*. Saint Louis, Missouri: Laumeier Sculpture Park
2003-04   *Mark di Suvero: Sculpture & Paintings*. Berlin, Germany: Akira Ikeda Gallery/Berlin
2001   Beasacier, Hubert. *Mark di Suvero*. Besanceuil, France: Galerie Bruno Mory
1998   *Mark di Suvero: Orange County*. Newport Beach, California, Orange County Museum of Art
1997   *Mark di Suvero – Paris*. Paris: Galerie Jeanne-Bucher
1996   *Mark di Suvero: The Hands*. Belmont, California: Wiegand Gallery
            Sandler, Irving. *Mark di Suvero at Storm King Art Center*. Mountainville, New York:
                Storm King Art Center
1995   Carandente, Giovanni, et al. *Mark di Suvero a Venezia*. Milan, Italy: Prada Milano Arte / Charta
            Mark di Suvero à Venezia. Venice, Italy: Gagosian Gallery
1994-95   *Mark di Suvero, Valencià, Spain*: Institut Valencià d'Art Modern, Centre Julio Gonzalez
1994   *Mark di Suvero*. San Francisco: John Berggruen Gallery
1993   *Mark di Suvero, Open Secret; 1990-1992*. New York: Gagosian Gallery/Rizzoli International
            Beasacier, Hubert. *Mark di Suvero: Extase. Brest,* France: Ville de Brest
1992   Bunk, Renate Luis, et al. *Mark di Suvero, New Star*. Stadt Viersen, Alemania
            Mark di Suvero. Nagoya, Japan: Akira Ikeda Gallery
1991   Dobbels, Daniel, et al. *Mark di Suvero: Retrospective*. Nice, France: Musee a'Art Moderne
                et d'Art Contemporain
1990   *Mark di Suvero: Valence.* Valence, France: Musee de Valence
            Mark di Suvero: Paris 1990. Paris: Galerie de France
1988   *Mark di Suvero*. Stuttgart, Germany: Württembergischer Kunstverein Stuttgart
1987   *Mark di Suvero: New Sculpture*. Tokyo, Japan: Akira Ikeda Gallery

1983	*Mark di Suvero: Major Outdoor Sculpture*. San Francisco: John Berggruen Gallery
1979-81	*Mark di Suvero*. Los Angeles: Gemini G.E.L.
1975	Monte, James, K. *Mark di Suvero*. New York: Whitney Museum of American Art
	Evrard, Marcel, et al. *Mark di Suvero*. Chalon-sur-Saône, France: C.R.A.C.A.P.
1972	*Mark di Suvero: Skulpturen im Freien*. Duisberg, Germany: Wilhelm Lembruck Museum
	Mark di Suvero. Eindhoven, The Netherlands: Stedelijk van Abbemuseum

awards & honors

1963	The Mr. and Mrs. Frank G Logan Medal for Individual Sculpture, Art Institute of Chicago
1967	National Endowment for the Arts Grant for Sculpture
1974	Skowhegan Medal for Sculpture
1983	The Arts Commission of the City and County of San Francisco Award for Distinguished Work and Achievement in Sculpture
1986	Elected to the American Academy of Arts and Letters
1987	Doris C. Freedman Award for Sculpture and Socrates Sculpture Park for contributions to the people of the City of New York that greatly enrich the public environment
1997	Named Commandeur d'Ordre des Art et Lettres for his significant contribution to the enrichment of the French Cultural inheritance
2000	International Sculpture Center Lifetime Achievement Award for contributions to the field of contemporary sculpture
	New York State Governor's Arts Award for Socrates Sculpture Park
2005	Heinz Award in the Arts and Humanities for contributions to America's cultural landscape through sculpture and an enduring commitment to broaden public venues for the visual arts
2006	Public Art Network Award for innovative and creative contributions and exemplary commitment and leadership in the field of public art

exhibition checklist

Drawings

Untitled, 1950, Pen and ink on paper, 13 ¾ x 16 ¾ inches

Untitled, 1968, Ink, pen and chalk on paper, 23 ¾ x 17 ¾ inches

Untitled, 1983, Gouache and felt pens, 35 ½ x 24 ¾ inches

Untitled, 1990, Ink and aluminum paint, 24 ¾ x 33 inches

Untitled, 1990, Ink and aluminum paint, 40 x 26 inches

Untitled, 1990, Ink and aluminum paint, 26 x 38 inches

Untitled, date unknown, Ink on paper, 22 x 30 inches

Untitled, c. 2001, Ink on paper, 22 x 30 inches

Untitled, date unknown, Felt pen on paper, 22 x 30 inches

Sculpture

Ave Delirio, 2001, Stainless steel and steel, 17'4" x 13' x 7'6"

Morfygon, 2002, Steel and stainless steel, 76 x 82 x 64 inches

Nextro, 2003, Stainless steel and steel, 57 x 73 x 36 inches

Arch Spirit, 2003, Stainless steel and steel, 27 x 22 x 47 inches

Potluck I, 2004, Stainless steel, 33 ½ x 19 x 16 inches

Untitled, 2008, Corten and stainless steel, 83 ½ x 57 x 60 inches

photography credits

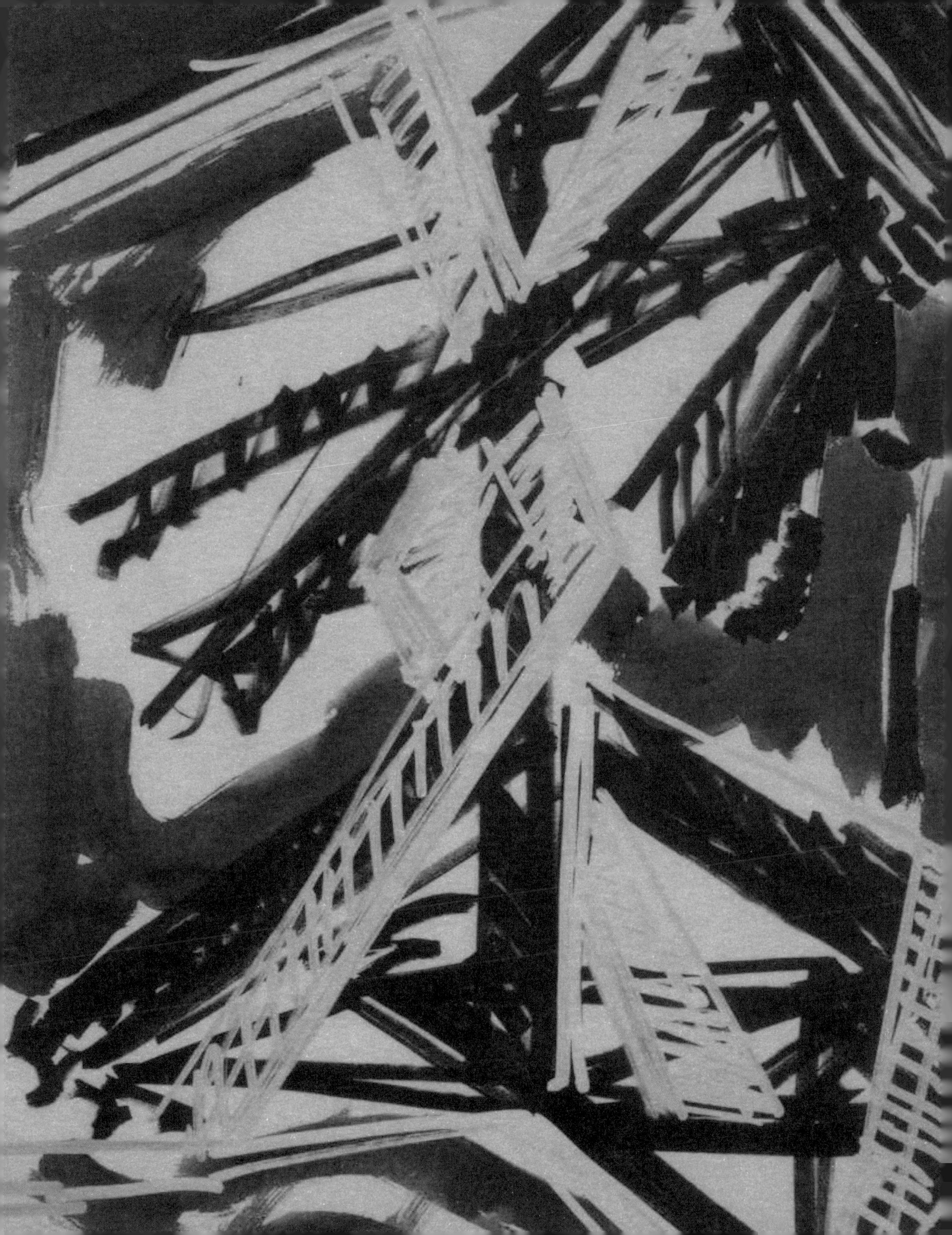

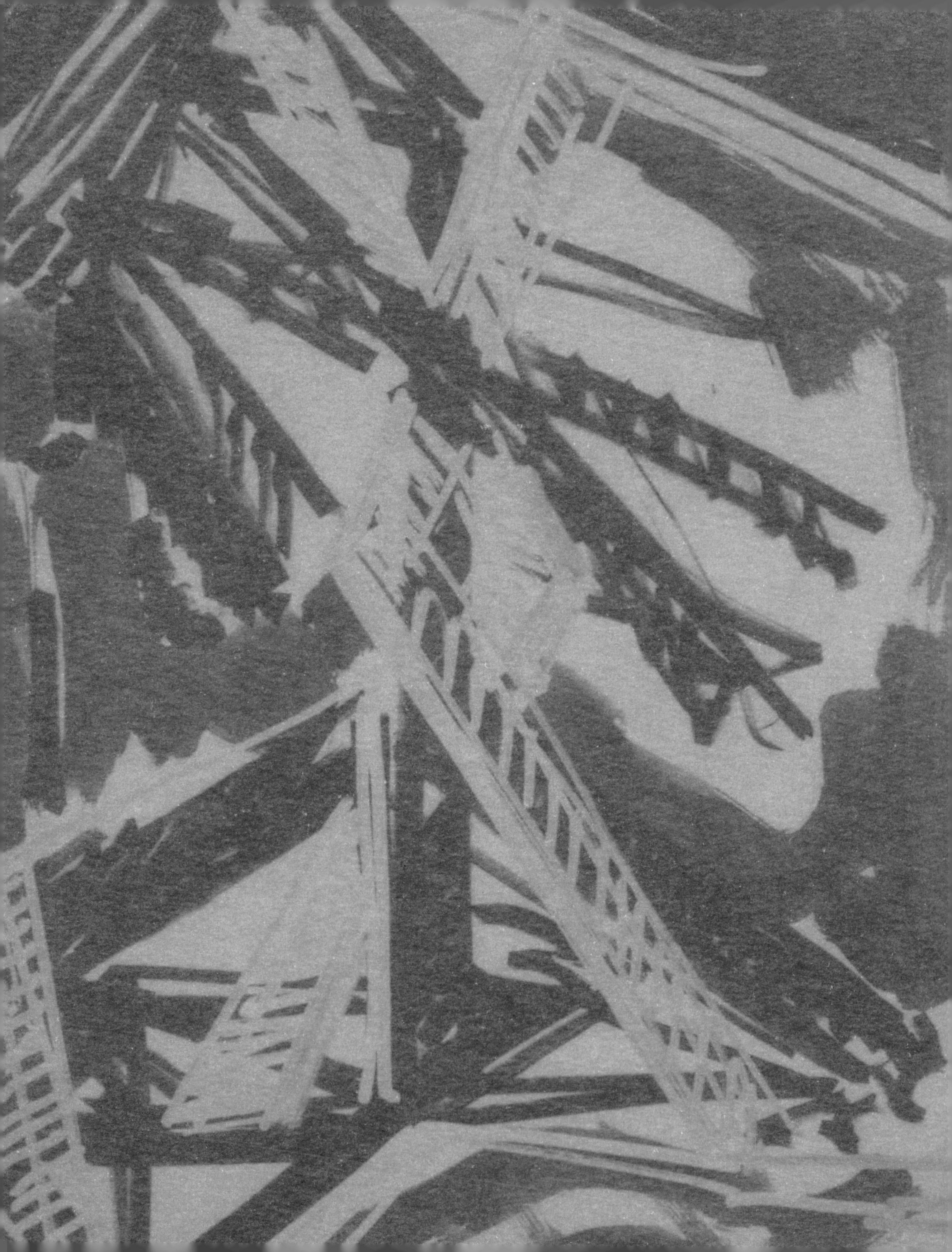